BOULDERING
ESSENTIALS

© 2018 David Flanagan. All rights reserved.
Published by Three Rock Books
www.threerockbooks.com
info@threerockbooks.com

Printed in Ireland
Walsh Colour Print

ISBN 978-0-9567874-1-5

All photos by author unless credited.

Front cover: Zlu Haller on the Rhino, Rocklands, South Africa. Photo by Zlu Haller. Back cover left: Jess Garland at the Castle Climbing Centre, London, UK. Photo by Aneta Parchanska. Back cover right: Kristen Ubaldi on Once Upon a Time, Black Mountain, California, US. Photo by Damon Corso.

BOULDERING
ESSENTIALS

By David Flanagan

Three Rock Books

CONTENTS

FOREWORD

Johnny Dawes is one of the most influential climbers of his generation, famous both for his audacious new routes and his unique climbing style. Throughout the late eighties and early nineties Johnny pushed the limits of bold traditional climbing with first ascents of routes such as Gaia, The End of the Affair, Hardback Thesaurus and Indian Face.

Considered one of the most technically creative climbers ever, Johnny moves with a distinctive dynamic style that was documented in the iconic film 'Stone Monkey'.

Nowadays, Johnny runs workshops across the world, sharing his unique insights into climbing movement.

I am a small chap so little rocks appeal to me. Even when some friends invited me to the Himalayas, which are brilliant, I found myself climbing on the boulders beneath Shivling, Shiva's old man.

Perfectly dry air, rock stripped solid, smooth here, rough there. What appealed to me most was the number of unclimbed strong lines. You could see how someone would climb them but not how on earth they could, for others there seemed no solution at all, holds missing, some holds too poor or misaligned.

There was one possibility that would require a run to use a smear to float beside two sidepulls that would induce a spin. Load that spin and the twist would propel you onto a big flat ramp just there, in the perfect position. Something never experienced before in the crimpiverse.

To the left another different in style. Get that flared pinch, undercut on that tips flake, paste your foot on an overhanging smear to latch an edge on a lip you must one arm mantel. What a collection of climbs it would be if you had a lifetime to spend at Tapovan.

Start how you want, do what others have done, but maybe have a peek around the corner, under the boulder. You might find a pot of gold. Hop, skip, jump or just try and hang on the unimaginable. You're free to do things how you want to. Climbs are a nonrenewable resource but new games are infinite. Bouldering was more of a toy when I were a lad but it makes a great strict discipline too.

My advice about boulder climbing would be to take your time. Sometimes I spend all day with students on the tiniest of boulders learning how to balance in the most tenuous of positions.

Know when you're really ready to move by buggering about, standing around even and when things get serious, painful and hopeful, you can listen to that now more familiar "yes" feeling in your head. The "A-haa" gland encouraged. Yes... Now! Try some smeary ones barefoot. You get more feedback with four hands... Train like a .... Too. Don't get strong get horribly powerful with fierce tenacity, clarity, fresh chalk. Come on try harder! It's in the sun do it later. Try the holds quickly. Your greasy fingered - mate give him a good book. Clean your feet. Clean your hands.

Don't always use a pad. You can get more problems done without one and the slight risk might perk up your concentration.

Above all surprise yourself. Enjoy more than you thought. Care more about your mates' success. Enjoy burning them off too. What's your cup of tea? Find out on those little rocks. Maybe it's the big rocks as it turned out for me.

- Johnny Dawes

INTRODUCTION

Climbing is a primal human instinct and bouldering, possibly with the exception of soloing, is the simplest, purest form of rock climbing. While soloing is high risk and only for experienced climbers, bouldering is playful and accessible to all.

Rock climbing is often incorrectly perceived as an activity that requires massive strength, but movement skills, creativity and imagination are just as, if not more, important.

Bouldering has existed in a very informal way since the late 19th century. And while it has always had its devotees, until recently most climbers considered it as nothing more than a distraction on wet days or as a means of training for 'real' climbing.

However, in the last two decades its popularity has surged largely thanks to the invention of bouldering pads and indoor climbing walls. Bouldering is now a recognised climbing discipline, a valid pursuit in itself with a proliferation of guidebooks, videos, indoor walls and competitions dedicated to it.

WHY BOULDER?

Bouldering is an excellent way to introduce beginners to rock climbing. It requires minimal equipment, it's safe and there isn't the distraction of ropework or fear of heights.

For route climbers bouldering is an excellent way to get stronger and improve their movement skills. It's also a good option when the weather is too cold to stand around belaying.

In these busy times bouldering is ideal for a 'quick hit' of climbing. It's a good use of limited free time, even an hour of bouldering is enough to get a workout.

Bouldering is the most social of the climbing disciplines, it's possible to boulder alongside others taking turns climbing, spotting each other, sharing advice and encouragement.

Bouldering, and climbing in general, is quite unique in that both sexes can compete on a reasonably even footing. In bouldering it's up to each individual to figure out a way to climb that is tailored to their strengths (power, flexibility, balance etc.).

THIS BOOK

This book has been written for beginners and intermediate boulderers, but hopefully even experienced boulderers will find some food for thought.

The initial chapters introduce bouldering to those completely new to climbing, before describing what equipment is required and how to stay safe while bouldering.

The movement chapter breaks climbing movement down into its smallest components and discusses each in detail, before moving on to techniques that involve the whole body working in coordination and discussing how these techniques are used on different rock formations.

The second half of the book deals with slightly more advanced topics such as bouldering outdoors, strategy, and training.

The final chapter describes some of the best bouldering destinations in the world.

FACING PAGE Peter Kußler on Suworow, Gotthard Pass, Switzerland. Photo by Rolf Seitz.

1

THE BASICS

Bouldering is climbing without a rope on boulders, cliffs or indoor climbing walls where a fall is unlikely to result in injury

Bouldering is the climbing equivalent of the 100m sprint. Risk, stamina, exposure and ropework are removed from the equation and the focus is on movement rather than getting to the top by any means. Bouldering requires and develops strength, balance, flexibility, coordination, determination and problem-solving.

Indoor climbing walls are responsible for a massive increase in the popularity of bouldering, and what was once a niche activity is now popular with both route climbers and those completely new to climbing.

The definition of bouldering is broad, as bouldering can mean different things to different people. It can be about pushing limits and climbing hard, getting outdoors with friends and having fun, discovering new problems or training for route climbing.

BOULDER PROBLEMS

A bouldering route is referred to as a problem. The term reflects the fact that getting to the top is as much about figuring out what to do as actually doing it.

At indoor climbing walls problems follow specific hand and foot holds (usually marked with tags or colour-coded holds). A problem won't necessarily go straight up, it may go across - a traverse - or weave over, around or under features, sometimes seeking difficulty, other times avoiding it.

Most bouldering is done on boulders and outcrops, but the base of larger cliffs and even buildings are used.

If the cliff or boulder is very high or the rock becomes loose or vegetated then the problem may be considered finished at a reasonable height rather than at the top.

SAFETY

Bouldering is one of the safest forms of rock climbing and serious injuries are rare. However, it should be considered low risk rather than risk free.

As boulderers don't use a rope to protect themselves they rarely climb high above the ground. The average boulder problem is about four metres high. This mightn't sound like much, but often the landing area is uneven or rocky and falls can happen very suddenly from awkward positions.

Boulderers minimise the risk of getting hurt in a fall by using bouldering pads and by spotting each other.

A bouldering pad is a rectangular crash mat that consists of multiple layers of foam covered in a heavy duty material. The pad is placed on the ground where the climber is expected to fall so as to cushion their landing.

Spotting is guiding a falling climber safely to the ground. The spotter's goal is to ensure the climber lands safely rather than to catch them in their arms.

Like most disciplines of climbing, risk in bouldering can be avoid or pursued. By choosing to stick to low problems with good landings you can stay reasonably safe or you can push your limits on high, difficult problems.

PREVIOUS SPREAD James Morris on Grandma Star Flash, Flock Hill, New Zealand. Photo by Troy Mattingley.
FACING PAGE Dan Varian on Where the Wild Things Are, Northumberland,UK. Photo by Dan Varian.

STARTING OUT

Nowadays, most people's first bouldering experience takes place indoors at a climbing wall.

Indoor walls are very popular with climbers for training, socialising and when the weather is too bad to climb outdoors.

And while climbing indoors is enjoyable and worthwhile, it can't match bouldering on rock. The contrast is vast, comparable to the difference between swimming in an indoor pool and the sea.

THE GOAL

Put at its simplest, the goal of bouldering is to get to the top. You may succeed on some problems on your first try while others can take weeks of effort. Bouldering has a strong sense of aesthetic, be it for the feel of a particular move, the architecture of a problem or the elegance of a solution.

Boulderers seek out problems that are enjoyable to climb, this may be because they take an impressive route up the boulder, have some really nice holds or very interesting movements.

Some problems reflect the playful aspect of bouldering, for example those that are solved by a running jump, a leap from an adjacent boulder or without using the hands.

CLIMBING WALLS

Until recently, climbing walls were the domain of experienced climbers but nowadays they also cater for beginners and people just 'having a go'.

Most walls provide a dedicated bouldering area, easy problems, coaching, good matting and equipment hire. This makes them the ideal place to get your first taste of bouldering.

Boulder problems are graded to indicate their difficulty. Don't fixate on grades, use them as a rough indicator of which problems you might be capable of climbing. Grading isn't an exact science, and grades can vary considerably between walls.

The best way to start is by seeking out the easiest problems and trying a few of them. On your first few visits you are better off doing a variety of easier problems than wasting all your energy struggling on one difficult problem.

For more basic movement advice see page 41 and for information about bouldering indoors see page 103.

EQUIPMENT

Bouldering doesn't require much equipment, to climb indoors all you need are climbing shoes and maybe some chalk.

Climbing shoes are tight fitting with soles of smooth sticky rubber that make standing on small or sloping foot holds much easier. However, they aren't absolutely essential, and most climbing walls hire shoes.

Climbers use chalk to absorb the sweat on their hands, you might find it useful as well.

Wear loose fitting but not overly baggy clothes. Walls can be cold so wear lots of thin layers so that you can shed layers as you warm up.

For more information about bouldering equipment see page 19.

SAFETY

Bear the following points in mind:

- The matting will cushion your fall but this doesn't mean you can't hurt yourself. Land upright, soak up the impact by bending your legs and rolling to the side if necessary.
- Don't wear a harness while bouldering.

- Remove any rings or jewellery, they could get jammed with very nasty consequences.
- Watch out for anyone underneath you while you are climbing and stay alert when walking around.
- Don't sit or lie around on the mats.
- Always give way to any climber that is higher on the wall than you.
- Children should be watched closely, they could be seriously injured by a falling climber.

BOULDERING OUTDOORS

After a few sessions at the wall you should be ready to boulder outdoors. The first step is to consult a guidebook, other climbers or the web to find an area with good landings and plenty of easier problems.

Ideally bring along a friend to spot and a bouldering pad. However it's possible to do some easy bouldering without either. Bring along a piece of carpet or matting to keep your shoes clean and climb close to the ground.

Bouldering outdoors takes some getting used to, so start off slowly on the easiest problems.

If there are other boulderers around they will usually be happy to give you a spot and offer some advice.

Remember to check the descent from the boulder before you set off, sometimes they can be tricky.

The one golden rule of bouldering is to never alter or damage the rock in any way. If you can't climb a problem as it is, move on to another.

For more information about bouldering outdoors see page 109.

FACING PAGE Diarmuid Smyth in Galway, Ireland.

THE BEGINNER'S MIND

"In the beginner's mind there are many possibilities, in the expert's mind there are few."
Shunryu Suzuki, Zen Master.

In Zen Buddhism there is a concept known as the Beginner's Mind. It suggests that those with knowledge and experience can benefit from adopting the lack of preconceptions and open, eager attitude of a beginner.

When we start out climbing it's fresh and exciting, the learning curve is steep and we are constantly improving. This rapid progress is exhilarating, but inevitably, it starts to slow down, the novelty wears off and frustration or complacency can start to creep in.

Any climber who can keep hold of the open, eager attitude of the beginner and combine it with their knowledge and experience, has a great chance of reaching their full potential as a climber.

MOTIVATION

In an activity where failure is such an integral part of the experience, motivation is critical. If you feel stuck in a rut, consider trying something different, a change of scenery - training at a different wall or visiting new areas - can be enough to refresh and re-enthuse.

PRECONCEPTIONS

A beginner's lack of experience also means a lack of preconceptions about the right way to do things. Every boulder problem is unique and there are often many subtly different solutions, so finding the most appropriate solution takes imagination and creativity. Relying on preconceptions can lead us down blind alleys or cause us to miss the solution entirely.

EXPERIENCE AND INTUITION

The Beginner's Mind concept doesn't reject or devalue the importance of experience, rather, it suggests keeping an open mind about how experience is used in new circumstances.

When you start climbing you rely heavily on your intuition and instincts, but as you progress, the focus tends to shift towards analysis. But it would be a serious mistake to ignore your intuition, after all it's just a subconscious manifestation of experience.

LEARNING

Beginners, aware of the limits of their knowledge, are happy to listen and take advice from others, however a lot of experienced climbers aren't so willing.

Rather than simply ignore advice, it might be better to listen and use your experience to decide which advice is worth following.

EXPECTATION

There is never much expectation on beginner's performance, the lack of pressure allows great freedom to experiment.

In contrast some experienced climbers feel heavily burdened with the weight of their own expectations and those of other climbers. This can make them reluctant to be seen to fail or perform badly and as a result they play to their strengths, which only serves to consolidate their weaknesses.

FACING PAGE Dave Flanagan on La Paillon Directe, Fontainebleau, France. Photo by Jeff Gardner.

2

EQUIPMENT

One of bouldering's many attractions is that it doesn't require a lot of equipment. All you need are climbing shoes, a chalk bag and, if you boulder outdoors regularly, a bouldering pad.

There are a few other less essential but useful items such as: a small patch of carpet or doormat to keep your shoes clean and dry before you step onto a problem, a tarp to protect your pad in wet, sandy or muddy conditions and a guidebook to help you find your way around the boulders.

If you are venturing off the beaten track, you should also take a map and compass, food, water, warm clothes and a head torch.

SKIN CARE

The following are worth carrying, especially on trips, to keep your skin in good condition:

- Finger tape - zinc oxide tape.
- Fine sandpaper or a pumice stone.
- Moisturiser.

See page 131 for advice about looking after your skin.

CHALK

Chalk (Magnesium Carbonate, $MgCO_3$) is a white powder that absorbs sweat from a climber's hands. Most boulderers find it indispensable as both a practical and psychological aid. While chalk doesn't increase friction, it prevents sweat reducing it (see page 118 for more information about friction).

Some chalk contains a drying agent that is helpful if you have sweaty hands or climb in a warm climate, but be careful that your skin doesn't become too dry.

Chalk is available as powder, chalk balls and liquid. Chalk balls are round mesh bags filled with chalk. While they reduce the amount of airborne chalk they aren't very effective and

the chalk tends to be very fine and talc-like.

Liquid chalk is a mix of chalk and alcohol that evaporates once rubbed into the hands leaving a good coating of chalk. It's useful as a base layer or if you can't use chalk (for example when training at home).

Use chalk sparingly, excessive amounts won't improve grip and non-climbers may consider rock that is caked in chalk unsightly.

Pof, dried pine resin that is wrapped in a cloth and slapped onto hand and foot holds, is used by a minority of climbers in Fontainebleau, France to increase friction. While its use in Fontainebleau is accepted by most locals, it's unacceptable to use it elsewhere. Pof destroys the rock by polishing it and makes the holds slippery.

CHALK BAG

A chalk bag (see above) is a small pouch for holding chalk, that is designed to be hung on a belt tied around the waist. When you can't or don't need to chalk up mid-problem leave it on the ground to prevent spillages.

Chalk buckets are large chalk bags designed to be left on the ground and they are more suitable for indoor bouldering.

An airtight bag or box is useful for storing your chalk and chalk bag as it tends to get everywhere.

CLOTHING

When you are bouldering a short walk from the car and the weather is good there is no need for any specialist clothing, but if you are walking to a remote area or expect cold or wet weather then the right clothing is essential to get the most out of the day.

- Hats add warmth without restricting movement. Make sure it covers the ears.

- Cold rock can numb fingers after only a few moves. A pair of gloves or mittens are the best way to get the warmth back into them.

- A breathable base layer with long sleeves will dry faster and keep you warmer than a cotton T-shirt.

- A fleece or wool jumper makes for a good mid-layer. If it's cold you might need to wear it while climbing so make sure it isn't too restrictive or bulky.

- When it's cold nothing beats a down jacket (*see above*), they are an essential item for bouldering in winter. A decent hood makes a big difference on those really freezing days.

- Nearly any trousers will do as long as they don't restrict your movement. Rolling up the ends gives a better view of the feet. In warm weather shorts will keep you cool but don't offer protection from rough rock, insects or undergrowth.

- It's rare to see a boulderer wearing socks under their climbing shoes, but if it's really cold a thin pair can work.

- Hiking boot are great for long walk ins over rough ground. They will keep your feet warm and dry, provide good support for your ankles and if looked after properly will last for years.

BRUSH

Excess chalk is easily removed with a brush (*see above*). There are a variety of fancy bouldering brushes on the market, however a plastic bristled washing-up brush works just fine.

Some climbers use a telescopic pole with a brush attached to the end to clean out of reach holds. Alternatively, just tape your brush to a stick.

Never use a wire brush as the metal bristles destroy the rock. For more about cleaning problems see page 121.

PREVIOUS SPREAD Nalle Hukkataival on The Swarm, Bishop. Photo by Reinhard Fichtinger.

SHOES

There is a wide range of climbing shoes on the market, many of which are designed specifically for bouldering.

When choosing the best shoe for your needs you must compromise between many different factors, such as:

- A tight fit gives better performance on small holds at the expense of comfort.

- The stickier the rubber, the faster it will wear out. Stiff shoes 'edge' well (see page 56) but 'smear' badly (see page 55).

- Thin soles are more sensitive but less durable.

Most beginners' footwork is such that their first pair of shoes don't last long, so there is no point spending a fortune on them.

Worn shoes can be resoled, but they won't perform as well as they did when new. One approach is to use a resoled or cheap pair indoors and reserve the good pair for rock.

Some boulderers find that one pair of shoes can't meet all their needs, so they own a selection of shoes, choosing the best shoe for each problem, sometimes even wearing different models on each foot.

FIT

The rule of thumb for climbing shoes is: the tighter the fit, the better the performance. Most boulderers wear climbing shoes a few sizes smaller than their street shoes.

Fit your shoes so that they are snug but not so tight that your feet are in agony, bear in mind they will stretch and mould to your feet to some extent (synthetic uppers won't stretch, lined leather uppers will stretch a small bit and unlined leather can stretch up to a full size).

Make sure that there isn't any dead space in the shoe, particularly around the heel.

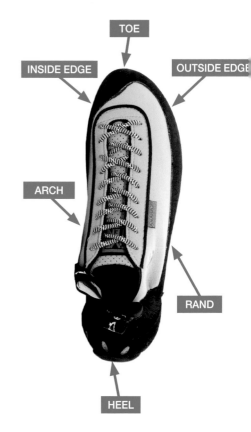

Shoes with thin soles and minimal lining perform best with a snug fit, while shoes with stiffer soles don't need to be fit too tight.

Remember that feet swell during the day, so it's best to shop for shoes in the afternoon.

Some climbers wear extremely tight shoes which force their toes to be clenched like a fist. This allows them to press down hard on small edges, but it can be a disadvantage on sloping holds where the goal is to get as much rubber as possible in contact with the rock. It's also not very good for the health of their feet.

Before you climb in new shoes wear them around the house for a few hours and if they

BEGINNERS/ALL ROUNDER

Entry level shoes tend to be stiff with a thick layer of rubber, flat soles and plenty of room in the toe area. And while not brilliant from a performance point of view they are comfortable and relatively cheap.

LACE UPS

Lace ups are the most popular style of climbing shoe. Laces are a little time-consuming to put tie and untie, however tensioning or loosening them allows you to adjust the fit. They are also very secure, which is important particularly when 'heel hooking' (see page 56).

VELCROS

Velcros have two or three velcro straps running across the front of the shoe, so they are quick to take on and off but otherwise they are very similar to lace ups.

SLIPPERS

Slippers were very popular in the nineties but aren't as common nowadays. They are quite soft and you need strong feet to make the most of them, so they aren't very suitable for beginners.

HIGH PERFORMANCE

High performance shoes feature an extremely down turned toe (for better edging on steep rock), very thin sticky soles and extra rubber on the top and side of the foot for 'toe hooking' (see page 58) and smearing.

BOULDERING PAD

Until the mid-nineties, when bouldering pads were invented, even short falls hurt. Pads have made falling off much more comfortable and have dramatically reduced the chances of injury. As a result the popularity of bouldering has soared.

Pads opened up problems and areas with rocky landings that previously could have badly injured any climber who fell. Nowadays it's not unusual to see a half dozen pads beneath a problem with a bad landing.

Pads not only reduce the chance of injury from a fall, they protect against long-term damage to the knee, foot and ankle joints which can result from repeated falls.

There are lots of different designs, but fundamentally a pad is just a few layers of foam covered in a hard-wearing fabric.

Most pads consist of a thick layer of soft foam and a thinner layer of hard foam. The hard foam is usually on top (i.e. the side you land on) as this spreads the impact which is then absorbed by the soft foam. On low, steep problems it can be better to face the soft foam up to soften a short fall onto your back.

Pads vary in sizes from small circuit or launch pads (1m x 1.5m x 5cm thick) to monstrous highball pads (3m x 2m x 15cm thick). The most suitable size depends on the type of bouldering you do, how big your car is, how long the walk in etc.

Very large pads have their uses, but most people will find two smaller pads more useful.

If you climb in a damp climate, it's worth removing the foam, placing it in plastic bags, sealing them up and returning it to the cover. This prevents the pad absorbing water if it gets wet.

The most costly part of a pad is the foam. Good quality foam that will stay stiff for a reasonable length of time is expensive. All foam has a limited life after which it becomes very soft, so if you use your pad a lot you might need to replace the foam every few years. While a pad makes a very comfortable camp bed, sleeping on it may reduce its life span.

If you boulder in remote areas make sure you buy a pad with well cushioned, wide shoulder straps and maybe even a waist belt.

TACO OR HINGE?

Bouldering pads come in two styles: taco and hinge.

Taco pads (*see bottom of facing page*) consist of one continuous section of foam that bends in the middle for carrying. The uniform surface of a taco pad means the landing area has no soft spots, however, they don't lie very flat on the ground. The cylindrical shape of a folded taco pad, while bulky, leaves space inside for carrying gear and most tacos have a flap to seal the bottom.

A hinge pad (*see top of facing page*) consists of two sections of foam joined by a fabric hinge. Hinge pads fold neatly and lie flat when open. And even though injuries caused by landing on the fold are rare, some manufacturers address this issue by using one continuous layer of hard foam across the entire pad or an angled or stepped hinge. Hinge pads aren't as good as tacos for carrying gear when folded.

There are a few inflatable bouldering pads on the market and even though they are heavy, expensive and bulky, the concept has potential.

3

STAYING SAFE

Bouldering is a relatively safe activity and serious injuries are rare, but precautions still need to be taken.

HIGHBALLS

Highballs are tall boulder problems, they occupy the middle ground between problems and routes. There is no consensus definition, some boulderers classify any problem over a certain height as a highball, while others say there must be a significant risk that a fall would result in injury.

As there are so many highly subjective factors a rigid definition isn't particularly useful. Perhaps it's best just to say that if a problem feels highball then it is.

Highballing is not recommended for beginners as, to be done with a reasonable safety margin, it requires a lot of experience, good judgement and a cool head. For more information about highballing see page 122.

MODIFYING LANDINGS

Some tidying or clearing of the landing area below a problem is common sense, but making significant changes to landings can be a cause of controversy.

What is considered acceptable varies from area to area and large scale disturbance may be frowned upon, especially by landowners. Use your judgement and consult other boulderers if you are unsure.

DOWN-CLIMBING

When you are high above the ground down-climbing is a safer option than falling or jumping. It's a skill that requires practice and certain types of moves such as dynamics (page 89) and mantels (page 78) can be very difficult, if not impossible, to reverse.

PLAN AHEAD

Spend a few moments before you start up a problem thinking about where and how

you are likely to fall. This will help you decide where to position the pads and spotters. As you make progress on a problem and learn more about the moves, reposition the pads and spotters as necessary.

LOOSE ROCK

Never let your guard down when climbing or spotting as you never know when a hand or foot could slip or a hold break. Give every problem, no matter how easy, 100% concentration until you have reached the top.

Holds typically break when you are pulling hard on them, resulting in very dangerous, explosive falls. Big storms and freeze thaw action can loosen previously solid holds. Some rock types, particularly sandstone, are fragile when damp so always allow them plenty of time to dry out before climbing on them.

Be especially wary of holds that have cracks around the edges or that sound hollow when tapped with the knuckles.

DIRTY ROCK

In all but the most popular bouldering areas you will encounter dirty or vegetated rock. Loose crystals or grains of sand act like ball bearings, causing the hands and feet to slip without warning. Moss and lichen have a tendency to hold moisture so vegetated problems will remain damp much longer than cleaner ones.

PREVIOUS SPREAD Ken Anderson on Jedi Mind Tricks, Bishop, California, US. Photo by Thomas Burden.
FACING PAGE Scott Archibald off of Saigon Direct, Bishop, California, US. Photo by Tony Symanovich.

FALLING

It's impossible to push your limits without falling, so it's an essential part of bouldering. Injuries from falls seem to occur almost randomly: some climbers are unlucky and break their ankle dropping a few feet onto a pad, while others walk away from massive falls onto terrible landings.

Landing with bad technique can lead to injuries but can also cause problems with your feet, ankles and knees in later life.

By making sure that you are familiar with the landing zone before you start climbing, you increase your chances of landing well even if you fall off unexpectedly.

HOW TO FALL

A 3m fall lasts just over three quarters of a second and you will be travelling at 27 kmph when you hit the ground. That doesn't give you a lot of time for conscious thought, you are relying entirely on your reflexes.

As you fall keep your torso vertical, your legs straight but not locked out, your toes pointed to the ground and your arms raised to reduce the risk of injuring your spotter.

Bend your legs as you hit the ground to absorb the impact, but avoid sinking into a deep squat position as it's very bad for the knees and you risk kneeing yourself in the face.

Your legs won't be able to absorb all the impact of long falls so as you bend your legs, drop sideways onto the pad with your knees, hips then shoulders. It's a little undignified but a lot better than a broken ankle.

FALLING ON SLABS

On low angled slabs you will slide rather than fall. Sliding is safer as it's slower and more controlled, especially on blank slabs where there is nothing to trip over. The trick is to keep your palms flat against the rock and to stay relaxed.

Another option is to turn around and run down the slab, this works well if the landing zone is large and flat but it has the potential to go badly wrong.

INDOORS

Indoor walls are a forgiving environment but you need to be constantly on alert for people walking or standing under you while you climb.

The wall is the ideal place to develop good falling technique, so rather than relying on the matting to absorb the impact, land properly (bending the legs and rolling if necessary) like you would outdoors.

JUMPING

Tactical retreat in the form of a controlled jump is often wiser than risking an out-of-control fall.

On steep problems it's just a matter of

hanging from the arms and dropping straight down onto the pads.

If the problem isn't overhanging, you will have to jump slightly outwards to make sure you clear the base of the rock. It's much safer to land facing the direction you are travelling (ie. away from the rock), so as you jump turn, push off with a hand if necessary. Practise this technique at the wall before you try it outdoors.

HELMET

Boulderers rarely wear helmets but there may be times when it's a good idea. John Sherman, American bouldering guru, wears a skateboarding helmet which he believes is better suited to the types of impacts in bouldering.

ABOVE Diarmuid Smyth greases off Marie Rose, Bas Cuvier, Fontainebleau, France.

PADDING

The thin, uncushioned soles of climbing shoes make even short falls onto anything but the softest ground uncomfortable.

Bouldering pads make landing more comfortable and prevent injury, so it's vital to put a bit of thought into where and how they are positioned as they aren't much help if you don't land on them.

Landing with part of the foot on the pad and part off can be as bad, if not worse, than missing it altogether. Very thick, stiff pads are the worst in this regard.

If the landing is sloped, secure the pad so it won't slide when you land on it. Tie one of the straps to a branch or root or wedge it in a crack.

There are rare occasions when you are better off without a pad as they can hide holes, obscure the best landing spots and give a false sense of security.

Even small voids underneath the pad can be potentially ankle snapping, fill any space underneath the pads with your shoes, rucksack etc.

POSITIONING

Don't fall into the trap of placing the pad under the start of the problem solely to keep your shoes clean and dry, think carefully before positioning it. Make sure that the pad isn't too close to the base of the rock, where it's highly unlikely you will land. Usually, the exception being low angle slabs, it should be at least a foot from the base and much more on steeper problems.

If the problem takes a straight line and the angle is close to vertical, place the pad at the base. But if the problem is steep or traverses and you only have one pad then it isn't so simple. You need to compromise between placing the pad where you are likely to fall and where it's dangerous to fall.

You may need to continually reposition the pads as you make progress on a problem.

Make sure the straps of the pad aren't sticking out as they could cause a trip or twist a limb if a foot tangles in them.

SPIKES AND ROOTS

A pad won't protect you from very sharp hazards such as broken branches or jagged rocks (*see top right*). So rather than covering them with your pad and forgetting about them, mark out 'no land zones' on the pad with a piece of chalk (*see top left*) or place some clothing or a shoe over them.

MULTIPLE PADS

Stacking pads is often necessary on high problems. Place the firmest pad on top and the older, softer ones underneath.

If you are faced with an uneven landing and only have a few pads, use the smaller ones to level the landing and fill in the gaps, then place the biggest pad on top to create a safe landing zone.

When arranging pads make sure that you don't create hazards such as small gaps or overlaps. Also, check that adjacent pads are of similar thickness and stiffness as the goal is to create a uniform landing surface.

FACING PAGE James Blay on Not To Be Taken Away, Stanage, UK. Photo by Paul Bennett.

SPOTTING

Spotting should be taken as seriously and done with just as much care and attention as belaying. A good spotter gives the climber the confidence to focus completely on the moves.

The primary goal of spotting is to protect the climber's head from an impact. The spotter isn't expected to catch the falling climber in their arms, only to guide them onto the pads, break their fall and ensure they land upright and in balance.

When spotting use a wide, firm stance with your hands reaching towards the climber's midriff. Stand a few feet beyond the point where you expect the climber's feet to hit the ground.

Focus your attention on the area just above the hips rather than watching the hands or feet and don't get distracted pointing out holds or studying the moves.

Once the falling climber reaches your outstretched arms, guide them to the pad and away from any hazards. Keep a firm grip on them until they have regained their balance.

On slabs and vertical walls the climber will either slide or fall with their body upright so all the spotter needs to do is steady the climber once they hit the pad.

On steeper rock the climber is likely to fall with their body at an angle and the danger is that they won't land on their feet. The spotter can help by making contact slightly higher on the falling climber's torso, rotating them into a more upright landing position.

Pay very close attention on problems that require foot cams (page 59), kneebars (page 61) or heel hooks (page 56) as if a limb gets jammed it could get seriously damaged, as well as tipping the climber over so they fall head first.

Some problems such as vertical walls with good landings or dynamic moves (see page 89), are potentially safer without a spotter.

If the pad is to be moved agree with the climber the best time to do it, ideally when they are in a secure position on positive holds.

Don't clutter up the landing zone by standing in the middle of it. If the climber decides to jump they shouldn't have to ask you to get out of the way.

MULTIPLE SPOTTERS

On some problems, especially those with stepped landings (see *facing page*), multiple spotters are essential. If you have two spotters on a long roof problem or traverse, the spotters should leapfrog each other so the climber has a spot at all times. Alternatively one can move the pads while the other spots.

When bouldering in a large group make sure someone is spotting before you leave the ground, don't just assume you have a spot.

DABBING

A dab is when, mid ascent, a climber brushes off or hits into their spotter, a tree, the ground, another boulder or a pad. This can be seen as invalidating their ascent. Some boulderers are stricter than others and even the gentlest touch will compel some to re-climb the problem.

As a spotter you should try and anticipate the climber's movements so that you can avoid touching them, but ultimately it's more important to spot well and potentially prevent an injury.

FACING PAGE Ricky Bell on Leftisim, Glendalough, Ireland.

4

MOVEMENT

Movement is both the foundation and the keystone of bouldering. And while it's possible to train hard, get strong and climb some hard problems, without good technique, you will never reach your full potential as a climber.

The temptation is to believe that improving is simply a matter of getting stronger and being able to pull harder on smaller holds, but a beginner's focus should be on learning good movement skills rather than building strength. This gives a solid foundation on which to progress as a climber and allows the muscles and tendons time to adapt gradually to the stresses of bouldering, reducing the risk of injury.

Even through every boulder problem is unique, some techniques and movements that occur frequently can be trained and practised, much like a gymnast trains on different apparatus.

This chapter describes techniques used by the individual limbs before moving onto movements that require the whole body. This slightly artificial approach is necessary, as launching straight into the more complicated movements would be confusing.

Familiarity with the basic moves and techniques of rock climbing is equivalent to knowing how the pieces move in chess. It's only a starting point for really learning how to climb.

Never be afraid to experiment and try new things. This is the beauty of bouldering, you are free to attempt moves that would be inconceivable on a route.

This freedom to experiment in safety and comfort - thanks to indoor walls and bouldering pads - has allowed the modern boulderer to discard the old 'three points of contact at all times' rule, and make frequent use of momentum.

However, there are situations when the old rule of "three points of contact at all times" is relevant, for example on highballs where a fall could be dangerous or when the holds are very small and your weight must be distributed over as many points of contact as possible.

IMPROVING TECHNIQUE

Even though climbing is a very natural, instinctive activity it still takes a lot of time and effort to reach your full potential as a climber.

Without a doubt, outdoor bouldering is the best way to learn and hone technique. Having said that, bouldering outdoors can be intimidating for an absolute beginner. The comfort, accessibility and variety of an indoor wall might be more suitable for an initiation, but don't wait too long before venturing out onto rock.

You won't become a better climber just by sitting on the couch reading this (or any other) book, but if you apply what you read about on these pages when you are out bouldering then you will be on the right path.

For more about training movement see page 142)

PREVIOUS SPREAD Jon Partridge on Lowrider, Stanage, UK. Photo by Nick Brown.
FACING PAGE Dan Varian on Bed of Procrustes, Millstone, UK. Photo by Nick Brown.

THE BASICS

Here is some movement advice for your first few bouldering sessions.

BALANCE

To climb in balance is to climb well. If you swing all over the place as you reach from hold to hold then you need to focus on how you are positioning your body relative to your hand and foot holds.

WEIGHT ON YOUR FEET

It's easier said than done, but unless the rock is very steep, your feet should bear the majority of your weight.

FOOTWORK

Your footwork should be deliberate, neat and quiet. Place your feet carefully and keep them still as you transfer weight onto them. Get in the habit of using the toe rather than the arch of your shoe.

A few small steps are better than one big one.

AVOID PULLING WITH YOUR ARMS

Your arms hold your body in balance, upward movement should come from the body's most powerful muscles, the legs. Ask yourself which is easier, a pull up or a squat?

STRAIGHT ARMS

Straight arms place the load on your skeleton rather than your muscles. Obviously you need to bend your arms to reach between holds but rest, scan for holds and move your feet with your arms as straight as possible.

DON'T ALWAYS CLIMB FACE ON

Beginners tend to climb with their hips and shoulders parallel to the rock but twisting your shoulders perpendicular to the rock extends your reach significantly and is particularly effective on overhanging rock.

PLAN AHEAD

Before you start up a problem decide which hand and foot holds you are going to use and in what order.

KEEP IT STATIC

Dynamics - jumping for holds - is a big part of bouldering but when you are starting out, aim to reach between holds in a smooth, controlled manner.

RELAX

Relax and don't forget to breathe. If your feet are pedalling furiously and your face is bright red, you are doing something wrong. Figure out what it is and fix it.

Make sure you don't over grip with your hands, it wastes energy when you need it most.

BE PATIENT

Good climbers can make hard problems look easy. It takes years of effort to get to that level, so be patient and enjoy the learning process.

Bouldering is difficult, that's the whole idea. Embrace the struggle and try not to get frustrated.

FACING PAGE Christian Prellwitz on Survey Marker, Sewemup Mesa, Colorado, US. Photo by Christian Prellwitz.

GENERAL CONCEPTS

The following general concepts are worth exploring before getting into specific techniques.

Some of these ideas are quite abstract, but a good understanding of them will allow you to solve problems intelligently, without resorting to trial and error, which is a highly inefficient (as well as unsatisfying) way to boulder.

For more in-depth information about the theory of climbing movement check out the excellent 'The Self Coached Climber' (see page 191 for details).

BALANCE

Balance in climbing is determined by the position of the climber's body relative to their holds. The term balance refers to the ability to maintain a state of equilibrium as well as to the state of equilibrium itself.

The importance of balance in climbing cannot be over emphasised. It is excellent body positioning that allows good climbers to do moves that feel physically impossible to other less accomplished, but equally strong, climbers.

Climbing moves can be divided into three broad categories depending on their balance requirements:

- Moves where it's impossible to compensate for a lack of balance with power, often described as balancy or technical.

- Moves that are forgiving of bad balance because the holds are positive and conveniently positioned.

- Moves that require good balance because they are close to the climbers physical limits and the climber has no power to waste on inefficient body position.

Steep problems that have large holds are very forgiving of inaccurate body position so it's important that climbers, especially beginners also spent time on less steep problems where good balance is essential and it's impossible to compensate using power.

DEFINITIONS

- The centre of gravity (CoG) is the theoretical point where the entire mass of a body is concentrated. Most climbers' centre of gravity is just above their waist near their belly button.

- The base of support is the area created by connecting the climber's points of contact (their hand and foot holds).

- Balance can be defined as the relationship between a climber's centre of gravity and their base of support.

Analysing this relationship between the base of support and the centre of gravity is a very useful way of understanding climbing movement and solving boulder problems.

However, this simple model isn't perfect, as it doesn't take into account the size and type of the holds. Positive hand holds are very forgiving of bad balance and allow virtually any position to be held, even if it means the centre of gravity is way outside the base of support.

RULES OF THUMB

The following rules of thumb apply in the vast majority of situations.

- The more time your CoG spends inside your base of support the more efficient your movement.

- The more points of contact and the further apart they are, the easier it is to make sure that your CoG lies within/on/over/under the base of support.

- Before you move a limb you must transfer the weight it's bearing to the other limbs.

- The more directly the CoG is over/under a hold the more weight will be on that hold.

STEEP SLAB SEQUENCE

The sequence on the left demonstrates how your weight must travel from side to side as you move from hold to hold.

1

A nice stable quadrilateral with the CoG centred in the base of support and weight evenly distributed between the two foot holds.

2

To free up the left foot the CoG is moved so that it lies directly over the right foot. The CoG is still within the base.

3

Once the left foot is on the higher hold, the CoG can be moved to the left to transfer weight off the right foot, so that it's now shared between the two hand holds and one foot hold.

DYNAMICS AND BALANCE

Climbing in balance is often equated with moving very slowly and deliberately, but dynamic (ie. fast) moves can combine balance and momentum very effectively.

Dynamic moves use momentum to get from one balanced position to another, passing quickly through intermediate positions where it's impossible or unnecessary to balance.

Static moves are generally done in two phases. In the first the body is positioned so that the hold is within reach, and then the reach is made with the hand (while the rest of the body, or the CoG at least, stays still).

In contrast, a dynamic move is one in which the CoG is moving towards the target hold at the same time as the reaching hand.

OPPOSITION

To hold onto the rock a climber must create enough upward force to counteract the downward pull of gravity. When they are using horizontal holds, this is straightforward as pulling straight down on the holds creates a force that directly opposes gravity.

However, when using vertical holds it's not quite so simple. This is because pulling or pushing on a vertical hold moves the body sideways rather than upwards.

So to hold the body in position, this horizontal force must be balanced by another opposing force. This pair of forces will be able to resist a vertical pull, much like a chain hanging between two posts.

The opposing forces can be created by:

- Pulling on a pair of holds that face away from each other, for example climbing a prow with one hand on either side (*see above*).
- Pushing outwards on a pair of facing holds, for example climbing a blank corner (see the photo on page 61) with a hand and foot pressing against each wall. This is known as bridging or stemming.

- A combination of pushing with a foot and pulling with a hand, for example laybacking a crack (see page 73) or an arete (see page 73).

WEIGHT DISTRIBUTION

The optimal body position is very dependant on the angle of the rock, but no matter what the angle the goal is always the same - maximising the weight taken by the feet.

On slabs (< 90°) your lower body should be upright so that your hips are directly above your feet (see photo on page 54).

On walls (~90°) your hips, chest and shoulders should be as close to the rock as possible. Not only does this force weight onto the foot holds, but it allows you to pull straight down on what are often very small hand holds.

On overhanging rock (> 90°) it can be difficult to keep your hips close to the wall, so focus on transferring weight down through the body to the foot holds by keeping the arms straight and the core rigid.

Roofs (~180°) are always strenuous, no matter how good your technique. All you can do is keep your arms straight and make the most of any toe and heel hooks.

BARNDOORING

A barndoor is an unintentional, uncontrolled rotation away from the rock (*see above*). When the base of support forms an approximately vertical line that lies to one side of the CoG, the body has a tendency to rotate. Depending on the exact configuration of the holds, this rotational force will either press the body into the rock or cause it to swing away (barndoor). The further your CoG is from your base of support, the stronger this rotational force will be.

Linear features, particularly aretes, are particularly prone to barndooring but it's possible in any situation. The tendency to barndoor is compounded when both your hand holds are sidepulls that face the same direction, as pulling harder will only make you rotate faster.

Once you start to barndoor it's very difficult to recover your balance, especially if the holds are marginal. So try and anticipate potential barndoor situations in advance and prevent barndooring by:

- Broadening the base of support by maintaining three points of contact during a reach. One point of contact should be off to one side of the linear feature.

- Keep your CoG as close to the centre of the base of support as possible. If you only have two points of contact use diagonals (left hand and right foot or vice versa) and try and keep your CoG below the base of support.

- Reach quickly so that you re-gain a stable position before you start to barndoor.

- Press your foot into the rock to prevent rotating. This is known as flagging and is described in detail on the next page.

ABOVE Dave Flanagan in Wicklow Gap, Ireland. Photo by Simon McGovern.
FACING PAGE Thomas Schmid on Atari, Bishop, California, US. Photo by Daniel Schmid.

FLAGGING

On overhanging rock small foot holds can be difficult to use, especially if they aren't ideally positioned. So, unless there is a profusion of large holds, it may be better to use only the biggest/best positioned foot hold. This allows you to position your body so that unhelpful movement is minimised as you reach and it also frees the dangling leg to be flagged.

Flagging involves using one leg to help with balance rather than using it to stand on a hold, much like a monkey uses their tail. It's a very useful technique, particularly on overhanging rock.

While flagging is primarily about maintaining balance, it can also be used to help a sequence flow or to generate leverage and momentum.

BALANCE

Flagging allows you to maintain your balance during a reach by creating a third point of contact that is positioned where it will resist barndooring.

Barndooring can occur when the base of support forms an approximately vertical line that lies to one side of the CoG. Pressing the flagged foot against the rock, on the opposite side of the base of support to the CoG, prevents the body rotating (*see photos 2 and 3 above*).

The flagged foot works like an outrigger on a boat, providing stability by widening the base and resisting rotation, rather than bearing weight.

FLOW

As you have only one foot on the rock when flagging, you only have one foot to reposition and the other is available to be used immediately. This makes moving quickly through strenuous sections quicker and easier.

Flagging from an outside edge (*see photo 3*) results in an almost identical position to flagging with the inside edge of the other foot (*see photo 2*), so in a lot of situations these positions are interchangeable.

This means that either foot can be used, presenting a wider range of options. This reduces the need for foot swaps, saving energy and helping the sequence flow.

LEVERAGE AND MOMENTUM

Flagging is one component of a technique called twist-locking (see page 71) in which

the flagged leg is used as a counter-weight that rotates the shoulder and the hand towards the target hold.

The flagging leg can also be used to generate momentum, by driving the leg upwards just before the hand starts to reach for the target hold.

TYPES OF FLAGGING

Flagging takes many forms and can be done with the flagged leg between the rock and your other leg (flagging inside) or behind your other leg (flagging outside).

Flagging inside (*photo 2 facing page*) is usually more effective as it encourages the body to twist so that the hips are perpendicular to the rock. Flagging outside (see *top right*) is used on very steep rock or when the foot hold is so high that there isn't room to flag inside.

If you have a choice whether to flag inside or outside, then inside is usually the best option.

Flagging from the outside edging with diagonal points of contact, known as a backstep flag (see *top left and photo 3 facing page*), is very effective, especially on steep ground, as it keeps the body close to the rock, maximising reach.

In photo 1 (on facing page) the climber has adjacent points of contact, and as soon as he moves his hand, his body starts to barndoor. In photo 2 his right foot is flagging inside, this prevents the body rotating. In photo 3 he uses an alternative solution, with diagonal points of contact, in which the right foot is on the hold and flags with the left foot.

Flagging is a complicated technique that can be used in many different ways depending as much on the climber's preferences as the problem itself. The only way to master flagging is through practice and experimentation.

TOP LEFT Niccolò Ceria on Murano, Champorcher, Italy. Photo by Rudy Ceria.
TOP RIGHT Dave Flanagan at Wicklow Head, Ireland. Photos by Peter McMahon.

HAND HOLDS

The following list describes the most common types of hand hold.

Some of the following terms can be used as both nouns and pronouns. For example a 'slopey pocket' or a 'juggy pinch'.

JUG

A jug (AKA bucket) is a large incut hold with a pronounced lip that is gripped with the whole hand (*see top left*). Jugs are generous holds that allow you to pull outwards as well as down which makes long reaches from them a lot easier.

EDGE

An edge is a flat horizontal hold (*see bottom left*). Small edges are known as crimps. A rail is a long continuous edge. An edge that is deep enough to sit on is called a ledge.

SLOPER

A sloper is a hold that slopes down away from the wall (*see top right*). On very rough rock like granite or sandstone even steeply sloping holds can be useful.

While strength is a factor, good body position and a strong core are vital to get the most out of sloping holds. The higher your body relative to a sloper the harder it is to hold, so keep your arms straight and your centre of gravity as low as possible.

POCKET

A pocket is a hole in the rock (*see bottom right*). Pockets, especially narrow, shallow ones, require a specific type of finger strength and good accuracy to catch and hold them.

A hueco is a large pocket, a slot is a wide, narrow pocket similar to a letter box and a mono is a single finger pocket.

CRACK

Cracks can range from millimetres to metres in width with parallel or flared sides (*see top left*). They can be jammed, gastoned, laybacked or avoided like the plague. For more on crack climbing see page 85.

PINCH

Typically a pinch is a vertical, symmetrical hold that is squeezed between the fingers and the thumb (*see bottom left*). Pinches vary in thickness from thin wafers to fat blocks.

Almost any hold can be pinched by pressing your thumb into the underside.

OTHERS

There are a few other holds that are specific to particular rock types.

A pebble is a tiny embedded stone - rarely bigger than a fingernail - common on gritstone (*see top right*).

On some types of granite the quartz crystals are large enough to be used as holds (*see middle right*).

Tiny protruding holds like pebbles and crystals can feel better if you stack your fingers on top of each other.

Cobbles are large stones embedded in the surrounding rock (*see bottom right*). They are found primarily on conglomerate but also on some types of sandstone. The cobbles are usually rounded and smooth. Check that they are secure before pulling on them.

HOLD ORIENTATION

The direction a hold faces determines how it's used and how helpful it is. A small hold in the perfect orientation is preferable to a large incut hold facing the 'wrong' way. Broadly speaking a hold can face one of four directions.

HORIZONTAL

Horizontal holds are the most straightforward. They feel best when you hang them with a straight arm with your body directly below the hold, this is especially true for slopers.

Unless the hold is very incut it will feel less secure as you gain height relative to it.

UNDERCUTS

An undercut (AKA undercling) is a hold that faces down (*see facing page bottom*). Opposition between your feet pushing down and arms pulling up holds you in place. Powerful arms, especially biceps, help on undercuts.

Most undercuts feel better the higher your centre of gravity is relative to them, this makes long reaches from positive undercuts relatively easily.

Undercuts can be difficult to spot from above so scan the rock at eye level paying close attention to the undersides of horizontal cracks and breaks.

LEFT Steven Sloan on Tri-Start, The Stone Fort, US. Photo by Steven Sloan.
RIGHT Dec Tormey in Poll Na Péist, Galway, Ireland.

SIDEPULLS

A sidepull is a vertical hold that faces away from the body (*see facing page top right*). They work best in pairs, both hands pulling towards the body creates opposing forces that hold it in place.

Problems that feature sidepulls are often very technical so balance and body positioning are more important than pulling power.

By leaning away from sidepulls and keeping your centre of gravity close to the rock you will avoid barndooring, which is an uncontrolled rotation away from the rock (see page 45).

GASTON

A gaston is a vertical hold that faces towards your body rather than away from it (*see facing page top left*). Held with the arm bent at the elbow and the hand, thumb down, pulling the hold away from the body. It's a very powerful technique and puts a lot of strain on the elbow and shoulder.

Some cracks can be climbed by gastoning with both arms in a position similar to that of trying to pry open an elevator door.

As your body position relative to a vertical hold dictates how it's used, a nasty gaston can be turned into a comfortable sidepull by shifting your body position.

ABOVE Rob Olsztyn on Marathon Man, Leavenworth, Washington, US. Photo by Ray Phung.

GRIPS

Finding the best way to grip most hand holds is pretty intuitive and straightforward, but on some complex holds, particularly outdoors, it can take a bit of experimenting to find the best grip.

The three main grips are open hand, full crimp and half crimp.

OPEN HAND

Open handing is when the fingers are only slightly bent (*see top left*). It's the most versatile grip and is the only option on large slopers and narrow pockets.

FULL CRIMP

Crimping is when the second finger joint is sharply bent (*see top middle*). It's very secure on small incut edges particularly if you place your thumb on top of your index finger.

HALF CRIMP

A half crimp is a compromise between open handing and crimping and is particularly useful on flat holds (*see top right*).

Open handing has a few major advantages over crimping.

- Gains in open hand strength translate to other grips whereas gains in crimp strength don't.

- Crimping is most likely to cause injury as it exerts large forces on the tendons in your finger joints.

- It's nearly impossible to grab a hold at speed in a crimp position.

- On rounded holds open handing maximises the amount of skin in contact with the rock.

Having said that there are times when crimping can be the difference between success and failure. However beginners should avoid it to reduce their chances of injury.

PINCH

Pinching is squeezing a hold between your fingers and thumb. Usually your thumb is on the side of the hold closest to your body, but occasionally bending your arm at the elbow and pinching with your thumb on the other side is more effective.

JAM

Jamming is wedging your hand or fingers in a crack. Boulderers tend to avoid it but good jamming technique can make some problems a lot easier. For more about jamming see page 85.

THUMBS

The thumb is the strongest digit and it should never lie idle.

A thumbcatch is when a conventional hold is supplemented by pinching with the thumb (*see facing page top left*). Even the smallest crystal or indentation can make a big difference.

A sprag is similar to a thumbcatch but the thumb pushes against the rock above the fingers rather than below (*see top middle*). It's even possible - usually on steep slabs - to undercut tiny holds using just the thumb.

CUSP

A cusp (AKA guppy) is a grip in which a protruding hold is squeezed, over the top or around the side, between the fingers and palm, with the fingers on the side nearest the body (*see top right*).

Some rounded indoor holds feel better when wrapped with the whole hand from the side rather than with just using a front-on grip. This also leaves more room to use both hands on the hold.

PALM

Palming is pressing the palm of your hand onto the rock. Palming with a straight arm pointing down onto a large hold can take a lot of weight especially on slabs or in corners. See photo on page 74.

POCKETS

Most small pockets can only be open handed or half crimped. For two finger pockets there are three combinations of fingers that can be used: front two (index and middle), middle two (middle and ring) and back two (ring and little). Which combination is strongest depends on the individual. On problems with multiple pockets it can be useful to use a variety of combinations to spread the load.

In some pockets it may be possible to fit another finger in by stacking it on top of the others. Remember that pockets are unique in that they can be used in any direction (ie. sidepull and undercut).

INDOOR HOLDS

The vast majority of indoor holds protrude from the wall so there is often something to pinch with your thumb. Sometimes the bolt hole can be used but this may be considered cheating.

MATCHING

Matching (AKA sharing) is placing both hands side by side on a hold.

SWAPPING HANDS

Sometimes replacing one hand with another on a hold is an essential part of the sequence, other times it's necessary because you make a mistake and are 'wrong handed'.

Swapping hands on small, narrow holds is a delicate operation that needs to be done one finger at a time. If you anticipate a hand swap, make it easier by leaving some room for the trailing hand.

INTERMEDIATES

Intermediates are small holds that are used briefly during a reach to a distant hold. See page 65.

FEET

Most beginners instinctively neglect their feet and concentrate on what their hands are doing. Needless to say this is a mistake, you can never put too much thought and effort into your footwork.

The best way to improve your footwork is to spend time bouldering on slabs, especially outdoors. Choose low problems with good landings where you can experiment free from worries about falling.

Attempting easier problems without using your hands will teach you a lot about balance and trusting your feet on marginal holds.

BASIC PRINCIPLES

- Place your foot on the best part of the hold at the optimal angle and don't look away until it's settled.

- Smoothly and confidently transfer your weight onto the hold. Jerky or hesitant movement causes slips.

- The more pressure you apply to a hold the better it will stick.

- A few small steps are better than one big one.

- The biggest foot hold isn't necessarily the best. Position is key.

- Make a mental note of foot holds while they are at eye level.

PREPARATION

Midway through a high step onto a marginal hold isn't the ideal moment to realise your shoes are filthy. Get into the habit of giving them a quick clean on your pad, a piece of carpet or your trouser leg before you pull on.

To maximise your shoe's grip 'squeak' them by spitting onto your hand and rubbing it into the sole until they are (literally) squeaky clean and dry.

Never put chalk on foot holds, it only makes them worse. If a hold is damp, dry it with a cloth or brush.

FEET LIKE HANDS

On steep rock you need to force weight onto your feet (and off your arms) by getting your hips close to the rock and pushing down and out with your toes as if you are trying to prise the hold away from the wall.

SWAPPING FEET

Often you will need to swap one foot for another on a foot hold. This can be a delicate operation especially on narrow or small holds. There are two approaches, the most common one is to do a little hop with the outgoing foot and place the incoming foot on the hold while you are airborne. On really delicate problems this isn't possible, instead gradually press the incoming foot onto the hold while sliding the other foot out.

SMEARING

A smear is a sloping foot hold, frequently smears are just a rough patch of rock rather than a clearly defined feature. Smearing can feel very precarious, staying relaxed and moving confidently will help your foot to stick.

Smears rely on friction so the more contact between the rubber of your shoe and the rock the better. Keep your ankles as low as possible and force weight onto your feet by getting your centre of gravity over them, bending you body at your waist so you can reach the rock with your hands (*see facing page*).

Soft shoes or slippers with clean, well broken in soles are ideal for smearing.

FACING PAGE Michele Caminati on Angel's Share, Black Rocks, UK. Photo by Adam Long.

EDGING

Edging is placing the side of your shoe on a hold. It's the most common and instinctive way of standing on most holds.

As when smearing you should try to maximise the contact area by keeping the edge of your shoe parallel to the surface of the wall and the sole angled so it's flush with the surface of the hold.

Edges on hard slab and wall problems can be really small, not much thicker than a credit card and they are probably the ultimate test of footwork (stiff shoes are helpful).

INSIDE EDGING

The straight edge running along the inside of the big toe is known as the inside edge (*see bottom right*). It's the most frequently used part of the shoe and is ideal for very small edges as it's so close to the big toe.

OUTSIDE EDGING

The outside edge (*see top right*) of the shoes is the section that curves around the other toes It's very useful on vertical or overhanging rock.

And while the outside edge isn't quite as secure or sensitive as the inside edge, it's will work on all but the very smallest holds.

Because using the outside edge encourages your torso to twist perpendicular to the wall, it's an essential part of techniques such as stepping through, flagging and twist-locking.

FRONT-POINTING

Narrow holds and pockets force you to use the tip of your toe rather than the edge. This concentrates all your weight on the end of your big toe and creates a lot of leverage on your foot.

Stiff shoes with a low-profile shape are best for pockets.

Front-pointing is also the best way to get as much rubber as possible in contact with the rock (*see top left*). Most smearing is done with the front of the shoe rather than the edges.

HEEL HOOK

Heel hooking is using your heel like an extra hand by placing the back of your shoe on a hold. Even very slopey or rounded features can make for solid heel hooks due to the heel's shape and the shoe's sticky rubber.

There are broadly two types of heel hook - high and low.

High (above the waist) heel hooks (*see facing page top and bottom and right*) take a lot of

weight and are indispensable in situations such as slopey lip traverses (see page 70). The hardest part is getting your heel in position. Good flexibility and a strong core help.

Low (below the waist) heel hooks (see top left) are more about maintaining balance than bearing weight. They are most common on vertical ground, for example hooking around an arete or on a vertical hold, acting like an extra hand to hold you in balance while you move a hand.

As your centre of gravity rises it becomes

harder to keep the heel in position, so the trick is to let the heel rotate so that you are using the side of the heel rather than the back (see bottom left).

A solid heel hook is as good as an extra hand hold so really pull hard to make the most of it.

TOP LEFT Nicky Bunn on Crossroads Moe, Yosemite Valley, California, US. Photo by Keenan Takahashi.
TOP RIGHT John Howard in the Cooley Mountains, Ireland.
BOTTOM LEFT Alex Germanovych on Dark Sakai, Magic Wood, Switzwerland. Photo by Nora Grosse.
BOTTOM RIGHT Valery Monnet on Le Toit du Cul de Chien, Fontainebleau, France. Photo by Christophe Sahli.

TOE HOOK

A toe hook is when you pull on a feature by hooking it with the top of your toe. Toe hooks are mainly used to maintain balance while a hand is moved.

On vertical rock sidepulls or aretes can be toe hooked, turning a desperate slap into a casual reach or allowing you to reach full stretch to the side. As a rule of thumb, if the hold is close to the body use a heel hook otherwise toe hook.

On steep ground toe hooks are used to prevent cutting loose (see page 71). They require constant pressure on them to stay in place. This takes good core strength.

It's also possible to get a toe hook high above your head, effectively climbing feet first,

however problems where it's the only solution are very rare (*see facing page top right and bottom left*).

BICYCLE

A bicycle (AKA clamp) is when one foot pushes down on a hold conventionally while the other foot toe hooks the same, or a nearby hold (*see above*).

Bicycles are most effective on horizontal roofs where the combination of pushing and pulling is more than the sum of its parts.

ARCH

The arch of your shoe is the curved area that runs from the ball of the toe towards

FACING PAGE Michael Perry on Murderboat Suicide, Lake Travis, Texas, US. Photo by Erik Moore.

the heel. Due to its curved shape it can be quite effective at hooking vertical features for balance (*see bottom right*).

FOOT CAM

A foot cam (AKA heel-toe jam) is an opposition technique that works well in horizontal cracks or breaks (*see top left*).

Place your foot into the crack and rotate your foot around your heel so that your toes press into the roof. This creates a very solid foot hold.

Because foot cams are so secure they aren't suitable for beginners. If you fall suddenly and can't free your foot there is a risk of very serious injury.

FOOT HOP

A foot hop is done when the next foot hold is too high to stand up on, it's equivalent to a dyno for the feet. Take a firm grip of the hand holds, spring off your lower foot and place your higher foot on the high hold. With practise this can be done very neatly and accurately.

If you find yourself doing a lot of foot hops you probably need to work on your flexibility.

TOP RIGHT Diarmuid Smyth, Three Rock, Ireland. Photo by Peter McMahon.
BOTTOM LEFT Dan Varian on Second Coming, Goldsborough Carr, UK. Photo by Ian Parnell.
BOTTOM RIGHT James Clancy on The Kerry Wave, Black Valley, Ireland.

LOWER BODY

Creative use of the lower body can turn a position that you are struggling to hold into a hands-off rest.

Some of the following techniques can be quite stressful on the muscles and joints so make sure you are well warmed up before doing them.

STEPPING THROUGH

Stepping through (*see above*) means standing on the next foot hold with the foot furthest from it (usually with your outside edge). It's very useful on traversing moves as it's more efficient than shuffling one foot along behind the other.

BACKSTEP

A backstep is when one foot inside edges while the other outside edges (*see bottom*). This turns the hips and shoulders perpendicular to the rock (facing the same direction as the knees point) making long reaches less strenuous.

FROGGING

Frogging is a way of getting your hips as close as possible to the wall by pointing your knees out to the sides (*see middle*). On vertical rock it's possible, if you are supple, to take a lot of weight off your arms using this technique.

TOP Paul Brennan on Milltown Bridge, Dublin, Ireland.
LEFT Diarmuid Smyth on Le Statique, Fontainebleau, France.
RIGHT Kevin Byrne, Bullock Harbour, Dublin, Ireland.

STEMMING

Stemming (AKA bridging) is pressing the legs away from each other to create opposing forces that hold the body in place (*see top*). It requires two facing surfaces (ie. a corner or groove) or protruding foot holds.

On rock with good friction even blank corners can be climbed using a combination of stemming with the feet and palming with the hands.

KNEEBAR

Use of the knee is generally considered bad style in climbing but kneebars are an exception. A kneebar is a jam that leverages between a foot and knee (*see bottom*). The foot is placed on a conventional hold while the knee (really the front or side of the lower thigh) presses into a corner, overlap or large protruding hold.

They are very solid, if a little painful, and have the potential to turn a very strenuous position into an opportunity to chalk up and rest.

It's possible to buy or make knee pads which can make kneebars a lot more comfortable.

LEFT Christian Prellwitz on Once Upon A Time, Yosemite, California, US. Photo by Christian Prellwitz.
RIGHT Trish Fox in Ayton's Cave, Dublin, Ireland. Photo by Trish Fox.

DROPKNEE

A dropknee (AKA Egyptian) combines elements of stemming and backstepping (*see right*).

As in a backstep, one foot outside edges while the other inside edges, but in a dropknee the leg using the outside edge is bent at the knee, which means that the feet are pushing out as well as down. This creates opposition, turns the body perpendicular to the rock and lowers the centre of gravity, resulting in a more balanced, locked-in position. This added control is vital when reaching for small or slopey holds.

Backsteps are suited to vertical ground while dropknees are more useful on overhangs.

A dropknee can be used in confined grooves and corners that are too narrow to stem (*see above*).

Deep dropknees (where the dropped knee is below the foot hold) can put a lot of pressure on the knee joint so watch out if you are prone to knee problems.

LEFT Tom Russell, Like a Bow, Albarracin, Spain. Photo by Alex Gorham.
RIGHT Diarmuid Smyth in Stuck Cove, Wicklow, Ireland.

UPPER BODY

Upper body movement is pretty intuitive and lacks the subtlety of lower body techniques such as backstepping or flagging.

TWISTING

On long moves, twisting (*see top left*) your torso towards the hold you are reaching from is more efficient than keeping your shoulders parallel to the wall. It increases your reach and as your locking arm is less bent it's also less strenuous.

However, when faced with a long reach to the side twisting isn't a good option as it moves the shoulder away from the target, and in that case you are better off keeping your torso parallel to the wall.

Combining twisting the torso with flagging and outside edging is known as twist-locking and is discussed in detail on page 71.

LOCKING OFF

A lock off is a static reach done with the holding arm bent sharply (*see top right*). They tend to be strenuous and are best avoided, but if the target hold is too poor or fiddly to lunge for, then you have little choice.

In contrast to dynamic moves, which are done in one fluid motion, lock offs have two distinct stages, firstly both arms pull the upper body as high as necessary and secondly one hand reaches while the other holds the body in position.

LEFT A Climber on Höhenrausch, Magic Wood, Switzerland. Photo by Rolf Seitz.
RIGHT Christina Pilo on Blacktop, The Tram, California, US. Photo by Susanica Tam.

CROSSING THROUGH

A cross through is when you reach to the next hold with the hand furthest from it (*see facing page*). On traverses it's an efficient alternative to shuffling the hands and matching every hold (see more about traversing on page 70).

When crossing through rotating your chest towards the target hold improves your reach. Whether you bring your reaching arm over (cross-over) or under (cross-under) your holding arm depends on the location of the holds.

It's possible to make very long horizontal reaches by bringing the whole body under and past the holding arm. This is known as a rose move after a move on a sport climb called "La Rose et La Vampire" at Buoux, France.

PALMING

On slabs even the smallest irregularity can make for a good palm and creative use of palming can get you up virtually hold-less corners and grooves. Warm-up well as palming moves are hard on the shoulders, triceps and back muscles. See photo on page 74.

GOING AGAIN

Going again (AKA bumping) is making two consecutive hand moves with the same hand (*see left*). If the first hold is only used briefly it's called an intermediate. It's useful when the first hold isn't good enough to reach from or when you need to get the second hold with the same hand to stay in sequence.

FACING PAGE Israel on Travesia de Loskot, Albarracin, Spain. Photo by Jorge Crespo.
LEFT Dave Flanagan in Glendalough, Ireland.

ROCK FEATURES

Familiarity with the common rock features will help you to plan your training, analyse your strengths and weaknesses (see page 140) and give you some idea of the types of moves and holds to expect before you start a problem.

The following list of the main rock features isn't definitive and there is often overlap between different features.

ROOF

A roof is an approximately horizontal piece of rock. Roofs place huge strain on the arms so it's vital to keep the them as straight as possible and get as much help as possible from your lower body using heel/toe hooks, kneebars and foot cams.

A long roof will test most boulderer's stamina to the limit, so it's vital to figure out a good sequence and move quickly. Getting into a standing position on the lip of a roof is often the most difficult part, this is known as turning the lip.

A short roof is known as an overlap and a rounded roof is a bulge.

For more information about roof climbing see page 82.

ABOVE Brian Hall in West Cork, Ireland. Photo by Richard Creagh.

ARETE

An arete is an outward facing corner. Aretes place similar demands on body positioning and balance as slabs.

Usually the best approach is to layback (see page 73) but if the arete is narrow or rounded it may be possible to climb it with a hand and foot on either side, squeezing hard to stay in place. This is known as compression (see page 74).

Aretes make for very striking lines and they are one of the most technically demanding features.

Overhanging aretes (known as prows) demand precision and power in equal measure.

ABOVE Diarmuid Smyth on L'Angle du Serac, Isatis, Fontainebleau, France.

CRACK

Cracks range in size from thin seams that just fit your finger tips to wide chimneys that you can easily fit inside.

Jamming involves putting some part of your body (fingers, hands, arms, knees, feet) into a crack and expanding or rotating it so that it wedges solidly. It can be painful, but once mastered it's very effective. Some experienced crack climbers claim a good jam is better than a jug.

Boulderers tend to avoid jamming, but for route climbers, crack boulder problems are the ideal place to refine jamming techniques before getting on the sharp end.

See page 85 for more about crack climbing.

ABOVE Lisa Bernard on Easy Street, San Diego, US. Photo by Ian Keirsey.

OVERHANG

Any rock that is steeper than vertical is referred to as overhanging. When the rock becomes closer to horizontal it's known as a roof (see previous page). Most indoor walls feature a lot of overhanging sections.

On overhangs not only is gravity pulling you down but it's also pulling you away from the rock, which means that you need to make an extra effort to get weight onto your feet and keep your body close to the rock.

Steep rock requires a particular style that combines twisting the upper body, flagging and using the outside edge of your foot (see page 80).

ABOVE Nalle Hukkataival on 'The Project Wall', The Grampians, Australia. Photo by Elly Stewart.

CORNER

A corner (AKA dihedral) is a feature in which two faces meet at roughly 90°. Corners, even very blank ones, are usually climbed by stemming. But if the corner has a flake or crack at the back where the two faces meet, laybacking is often the best option.

A lot of techniques for climbing corners can come in handy in any situation where there are protruding holds.

ABOVE Katy Whittaker on King Cobra, Yosemite, California, US. Photo by Ryan Pasquill.

SLAB

A slab is a section of rock angled at less than vertical. Holds on slabs are small and depending on the type of rock, there may be tiny edges, pebbles, crystals or smears.

Slabs respond well to a slow, methodical, confident approach. Stamina and strength are of little relevance, balance, strong legs and good footwork are the crucial factors.

As they don't require much pulling from the arms and fingers they are a good option when recovering from an injury or tired. And slab climbing is, without a doubt, the best method of improving your footwork.

ABOVE Lee Robinson on St. Kevin's Slab, Wicklow, Ireland. Photo by Lisa Robinson.

WALL

A wall (AKA face) is an approximately vertical piece of rock. The hand holds are usually small but unlike slab climbing it's often necessary to pull hard on them rather than just use them for balance.

Flexibility, strong fingers and good balance are vital skills for climbing vertical rock.

ABOVE Damon Corso on Da Light, Doolin, Ireland. Photo by Damon Corso.

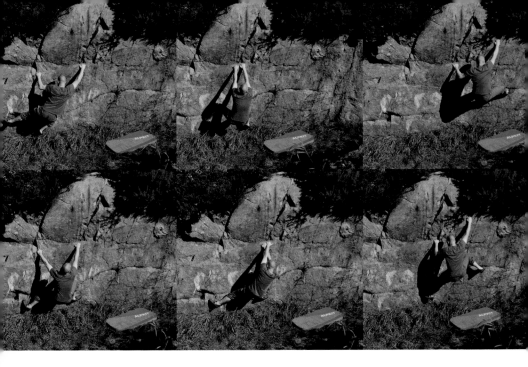

FULL BODY MOVEMENT

Now that the use of each limb has been considered in isolation, it's time to bring everything together and describe moves that involve the whole body.

TRAVERSING

Traversing is climbing sideways, it can be done in two different ways: shuffling and crossing.

Shuffling (*see top*) is reaching to the next hold with the hand/foot closest to it before bringing the other hand/foot onto the hold just vacated. It minimises the length of each reach which can be critical if the holds are small.

Crossing (*see bottom*) involves crossing through with the hands (page 65) and/or stepping through with the feet (page 60). It's efficient as it eliminates matching and minimises the number of moves.

You may take one approach with the hands and the other with the feet or change approach between moves. It can take time to find out the best sequence for a traverse, but as you can start at any point, they are suited to experimentation.

HEEL HOOK TRAVERSING

Heel hooking is a very effective way to tackle isolated linear features such as a slopey arete, ledge or the lip of a roof. Your hands shuffle or cross over while one foot heel hooks and the other foot flags, smears or uses holds on the underside of the feature.

Most heel hook traverses are climbed hands first, but leading with the feet, even for just a move or two, can work well in some cases.

If you need to cut loose to reset your feet use the momentum of the swing to reposition them rather than killing the swing only to have to bring your feet back up.

It's tempting to move your hands as far as possible before moving your feet, but the greater the gap between hands and feet, the harder it is to move. Short, frequent readjustments are best.

Look out for situations when a toe hook or smearing the arch is a better option than a heel hook.

ABOVE Dave Flanagan, Dalkey Quarry, Ireland.

CUTTING LOOSE

Cutting loose is when both feet swing off the rock and all your weight is taken by the hand holds (*see left*).

Usually cutting loose is caused by a loss of body tension while climbing steep rock on small foot holds. But there are times when it's done intentionally, for example to use the momentum of the swing to get a heel hook on the lip of a roof.

When facing an inevitable cut loose, rather than releasing both feet simultaneously, release and dangle the least solid foot before releasing the other. This reduces the force of the swing considerably.

To prevent cutting loose, press hard on the foot holds and keep your core tense. Avoid letting your body get too spread out as the greater the distance between your hands and feet the harder it is to keep pressure on your feet. Plus if they do cut loose the swing will be bigger and harder to control.

TWIST-LOCKING

Twist-locking is a very efficient way to make long reaches on steep ground that combines twisting the shoulders, flagging and outside edging (*see right*).

By twisting your shoulders perpendicular to the rock (with your chest facing your lower arm) you maximise your reach and keep your lower arm relatively straight.

Standing on the outside edge of your foot facilitates this twisting motion, and flagging with the other leg further encourages the torso to twist as you reach.

LEFT Blaine Burns at Lake Travis, Texas, US. Photo by Erik Moore.
RIGHT Ellen Alger at Lake Travis, Texas, US. Photo by Erik Moore.

LAYBACKING

Laybacking (AKA liebacking) is a technique for climbing continuous vertical features (such as cracks, flakes or aretes). Pulling with the hands and pushing with the feet create opposing forces that hold the body in place.

Generally speaking laybacking up cracks/corners/flakes is strenuous while laybacking aretes is more about balance.

CRACK/CORNER/FLAKE

When laybacking a crack, corner or flake the feet press on the far lip (or the opposite wall if the crack is in a corner) while the hands pull on the near side of the feature (see facing page).

The higher the feet relative to the hands the more secure the position will be. However it will also be more strenuous, so move quickly, especially when there aren't any good foot holds.

ARETE

Arete laybacking (see left) is all about footwork and body position. Your body must lean away from the arete to create opposition between your hands, which are pulling the arete, and your feet, which are pushing. It's vital to get your centre of gravity as close to the rock as possible, to prevent barndooring (see page 45), especially on slopey aretes.

Heel or toe hooking with the foot closest to the arete is an ideal way to maintain balance while moving a hand or chalking up, they work best if the other foot outside edges.

As when traversing, you have a choice between shuffling or crossing your hands. However, on delicate aretes crossing usually isn't an option.

Once you have started up an arete it's difficult to locate holds on the other side so make a mental note of them before you start climbing. Look out for small hand holds on the face as they can be very helpful for balance (see right).

FACING PAGE Chris Tartaglia on Year of the Dragon, Flock Hill, New Zealand. Photo by Tom Hoyle.
LEFT Michele Caminati on Ulysses, Stange, UK. Photo by Paul Bennett.
RIGHT Jeff Gardner on Solidarity, Wicklow, Ireland. Photo by Diarmuid Smyth.

FRICTION SLABS

On blank, low angled slabs technique is everything, strength is irrelevant as there aren't any holds to pull on.

When climbing friction slabs makes sure that your centre of gravity is over your feet, your heels are kept low and your palms are pressed flat against the rock (see photo on page 54 and top left).

Long reaches shift your centre of gravity forward, which transfers weight off your feet, potentially causing them to slip (the more weight you put on a foot hold the better it will stick). Gain height gradually, using small steps, shifting your weight smoothly and confidently from one smear to the next.

BLANK CORNERS

Blank corners and grooves are best climbed by using a combination of stemming (page 61) with the legs and palming with the hands (see top right).

If the distance between holds or surfaces is too wide to stem with the legs the only alternative is to span the gap with the hands on one side and feet on the other. This is known as a full body stem and is very rarely necessary (see photo on page 86).

There are problems which are easier if climbed facing outwards but the vast majority of the time you should face the rock.

COMPRESSION

Compression is using both hands and feet (often heel or toe hooking) to squeeze a feature (see facing page). Each hold is useless on its own, but when combined with opposing holds, it's possible to hang on. Because of this, hand movements must be done very quickly and aggressively.

Compression problems, especially those that tackle steep and slopey prows or roofs, are much sought after by modern boulderers.

LEFT Dave Flanagan, Wicklow, Ireland. Photo by Simon McGovern.
RIGHT Christian Prellwitz on Streetcar Named Desire, Joshua Tree, California, US. Photo by Christian Prellwitz.
FACING PAGE Zac Orme on Conan, Castle Hill, New Zealand. Photo by Derek Thatcher.

ROCKOVER

A rockover is when you place a foot on a high foot hold and stand up on it using a combination of pulling with the arms and pushing with the legs.

Rockovers require powerful leg muscles (strengthen them with squats or pistols, see page 156), balance and coordination. They are most common on vertical and slabby ground.

Some rockovers must be done very slowly, pressing inch by inch, while others are easiest if they are done quickly, almost like the start of a dynamic move.

1
Place your foot, usually the toe but sometimes the heel (see page 79), on the high foot hold. Get your hands as high as possible.

2
With help from your arms shift your weight onto the higher foot hold.

3
Smoothly press your leg and push down on the hand holds, usually the hardest part is getting the movement started.

Your lower leg will leave its foot hold and in some situations, especially very slow grinding rockovers, it can be helpful to drag it against the rock as a sort of ratchet to ensure you don't lose any ground.

TOP Dave Flanagan at Awesome Walls, Dublin, Ireland.
BOTTOM Paul Brennan on Milltown Bridge, Dublin, Ireland.

TOPPING OUT

At most indoor walls you jump or climb down from the final holds of each problem, but at most outdoor bouldering areas a problem isn't considered finished until you are standing on top of the boulder or cliff. This process of getting established on the top of a problem is known as topping out.

Certain rock types, particularly granite and sandstone, tend to have very smooth, rounded tops. This can mean that even if finishing the problem isn't technically the crux, it can feel that way thanks to the height and the fact that you are tired when you get there.

On top outs there is no substitute for good technique so beware of falling into the trap of watching an experienced climber effortlessly finish a problem and assuming that you will find it just as easy.

Practise the various topping out techniques on plenty of low problems before testing yourself on higher ones. This is especially important for climbers who don't have much experience of bouldering outdoors. Even relatively easy top outs can feel strenuous, insecure and scary if your technique is rusty.

If you think the top out is going to be difficult it can be well worth inspecting it from above, locating any useful holds and maybe giving them a quick brush.

Mantling (see page 78) is the most efficient way to top out but if the top is rounded and lacks holds you may need to rockover onto your heel (see page 79).

If nothing else works, the very last resort is to do a 'beached whale', this involves flopping over the top onto your stomach and kicking your feet and wriggling your body until you can stand up. It isn't a very effective or elegant technique, but it's guaranteed to entertain any onlookers.

ABOVE John Howard topping out in Glenmacnass, Ireland. Photo by Matt Davis.

MANTEL

Mantling is a method of getting from hanging from a feature to standing on it, without help from any higher holds. Mantels are similar to rockovers, but the arms rather than the legs do the pushing.

Mantels are commonly encountered when topping out, but may also be required mid-problem on ledges or large flat holds. The approach is similar but can be complicated if the rock above the ledge prevents you leaning in and getting weight onto your palms.

Press ups and dips (see page 156) strengthen the pushing muscles such as the deltoids and triceps that are critical for mantling.

1

Once you reach the lip decide which hand you are going to palm down with first. If one side of the lip is higher or more positive choose that hand, otherwise, use your preferred hand. Place one foot high enough that your waist will be level with your hands when you stand up.

If possible combine steps 2 and 3 into one smooth motion.

2

Simultaneously pull your shoulders towards the lip and stand up on the high foot hold. As your shoulders rise above the lip rotate your chosen hand so its fingers face the other hand and your palm is flat on the rock. At this stage your arm will be sharply bent with your elbow pointing up in the air.

3

Straighten the bent arm and as soon as possible rotate your other hand so the fingers of each hand face each other. Keep pressing until both arms are straight.

4

Bring a foot onto the lip and lean forward to shift weight onto it. Move your inside hand forward and bring the other foot up.

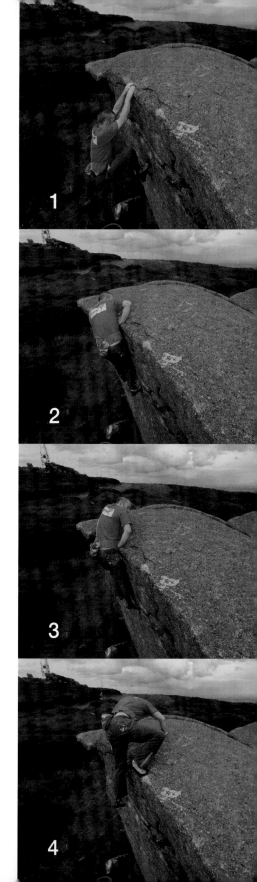

HEEL ROCKOVER

Blank, rounded or undercut top outs are best tackled with an approach that combines elements of rocking over and mantling.

Tackled decisively with good technique these top outs aren't that bad, but if you lose your nerve midway they can get messy.

Palming down is essential so don't be distracted by small holds near the lip.

1

Start with your feet. high, level with your waist if possible, and pull with the arms just enough to allow you to get a good heel hook on the lower side of the lip.

Steps 2,3 and 4 should be done in one smooth motion.

2

Pull with your arms and heel and push with your lower foot. Once your waist is close to the lip, turn your inside hand so the fingers face your other hand and the palm is flat on the rock.

3

Continue pressing down with your palm. As your waist rises above the lip lean forward to transfer more weight onto the palm and change your heel hook to a smear.

4

Straighten both your arms, move your foot closer to your body and bring your other foot onto the lip. This position is quite precarious so pay close attention to your balance.

FACING PAGE AND LEFT Dave Flanagan, Three Rock, Ireland.

STEEP GROUND

The most effective way to climb steep rock (overhanging between 10° and 45°) is to use a combination of twist-locking, flagging, stepping through, outside edging and dropknee-ing.

More than any other angle, flow and continuity are required on steep ground. As the holds are small and good rests rare, the fastest solution is usually the best one.

To become fluent in this style practice is vital. Start off on big holds and get a good understanding of the basic movements before moving onto harder problems with long moves between small or slopey holds.

Each move in the sequence should flow logically into the next with the body twisting from one side to the other.

The following sequence demonstrates how some of the common steep ground techniques can be combined.

1
Sit start with the left foot outside edging and the right inside edging.

2
Right hand is reset higher to set up for the long reach to the left. Right foot flags.

3
The shoulders are parallel (rather than perpendicular) to the rock to maximise horizontal reach. Room is left on the hand hold so that it can be matched with the other hand. Another more powerful option would be to cross the right hand over the left.

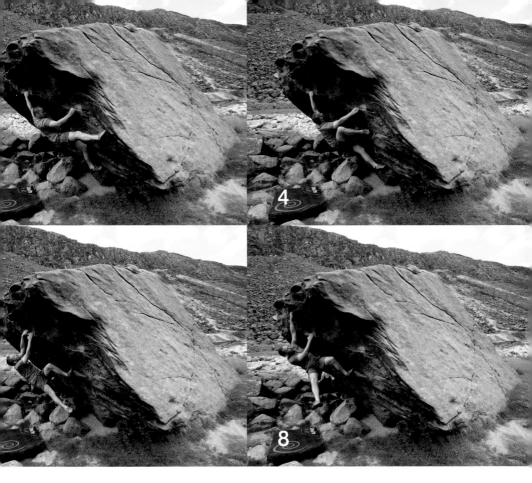

4

The right foot gets a side heel hook on the starting hand hold.

5

The hold is matched keeping both arms as straight as possible.

6

After the match the left foot outside edges on the starting hold while both arms are kept straight.

7

The right foot flags. Another option would be to use the right foot on the starting hold and flag inside with the left foot.

8

Moving the flagged foot away from the rock increases the leverage, helping the shoulders twist towards the next hold and allowing the right arm to stay relatively straight.

ABOVE Dave Flanagan on the back of Big Jim, Glendalough, Ireland.

ROOFS

Roof climbing is strenuous so don't hang around, move quickly and decisively. There is no point try to rest or recover mid-roof unless you find a very good hands-free rest.

It's vital to keep your arms straight as they will bear the majority of your weight and will burn out very quickly if they are constantly bent.

Tricks such as climbing feet first, rotating one way then the other, kneebars, heel hooks, toe cams and bridging are all commonly used, especially on featured roofs which offer vast possibilities in all three dimensions.

Use your feet like hands, actively gripping holds rather than just passively standing on them. Any weight you can take off your arms through clever use of your feet is a bonus, but the priority is to anchor your body and prevent cutting loose (see next page).

Once you have pulled onto the start of a roof problem it's usually difficult to see holds over the lip, so make a mental note of their location before you start climbing.

Even though technically speaking a roof is a horizontal section of rock, once the rock overhangs by more than 45° you may need to use roof climbing techniques.

Most roof problems are short, no more than a body length long, and often the most strenuous part is turning the lip.

1

A powerful reach from a small finger pocket on the underside of the roof leads to a larger pocket on the lip.

A staggered foot position, with one foot high and one low helps shift weight from the lower to the higher foot during the reach.

Another option would be to get a heel hook on the rounded jug at the back of the roof. This would take weight off the arms and prevent cutting loose mid-reach.

2

Upon reaching the pocket on the lip with a straight arm, the feet are reset and the other hand is brought briefly to the lip.

At this point the body is quite spread out and a lot of body tension is required to hold it in place.

3

A twist-lock (see page 71) is used to reach the next hold, using the outside edge of the right foot and flagging with the left foot.

If there is no suitable foot holds for a twist-lock, either get a heel hook on the lip or just jump for the next hold. The last resort is to campus (see page 101).

4

Faced with a lack of foot holds and a long reach to the next hold, there is no option but to jump. The momentum of the swing is used to reset the feet.

5

While keeping the arms as straight as possible a foot hold is selected just over the lip.

It shouldn't be too close to the body or it will be awkward to get the foot on it, but if it's too far away it will be harder to rock over onto.

Ideally the foot hold should be on the same side as the reaching hand to give a strong diagonal.

6

A hard pull with the arms while rocking over onto the foot hold brings the top within reach.

Getting the other foot on a hold above the lip is important, but isn't necessary in this case as the top is within reach.

ABOVE Jacob Cook on Le Toit du Cul de Chien, Fontainebleau, France. Photo by Peter Wilkinson.

CRACK CLIMBING

Crack climbing is probably the most specialised type of climbing. A crack's difficulty can also be very specific to the climber's morphology, particularly the size of their hands and fingers. Some cracks are almost impossible without the right technique.

Boulderers, as a rule, don't gravitate towards cracks, but the basic principles are worth mentioning as they can be helpful in a variety of other situations. For example, a hand jam at the back of a slopey break can allow you to rest when you would struggle just to hang on using more conventional technique.

However, crack climbing skills are by no means essential for the boulderer and laybacking, gastoning or bridging should suffice on the majority of cracks encountered.

For more detailed information about crack climbing check the references (page 191).

JAMMING

When jamming, look for constrictions in the crack where your fingers/hands will wedge naturally. In parallel cracks you need to twist the fingers/hands to create enough force to hold you in place.

Jamming can be very hard on the skin, most damage is done when a jam slips, so make sure the jam is well set before you put any weight on it. If you are doing a lot of jamming on rough rock it might be worth taping your hands.

FINGER CRACKS

Finger cracks are jammed by placing the fingers in the crack, usually with the thumb pointing down (however pointing the thumb up allows longer reaches) and twisting the hand until the fingers lock. Finger jamming is painful and it's one of the hardest jams to master.

HAND CRACKS

The hand is inserted into the crack, knuckles against one side, finger tips and palm against the other (*see middle left and bottom of facing page*). Opposition is created by squeezing the thumb behind the palm rather than pushing with the fingers.

FIST CRACKS

To fist jam place your hand across the width of the crack (facing in or out) and clench your hand (*see top left of facing page*). The width of the crack dictates whether your thumb should be inside or outside your fist.

FOOT JAMMING

In narrow cracks foot jam by inserting your foot into the crack with the sole parallel to the sides and twisting so it lodges solidly (*see top right of facing page*).

Wider cracks require a heel-toe jam, which is done with the foot angled diagonally down and the heel pressing against one side while the toes press against the other. Heel-toe jams are essentially a foot cam (see page 59) done in a vertical rather than horizontal crack.

Foot jams can often be found on problems with no other jamming as the foot will stick in places too flared or wide for the hands.

Be very careful when foot jamming, if your hands slip and your feet remain in place you risk serious injury.

FACING PAGE TOP RIGHT Chris Fryer in Quantum Fields, Castle Hill, New Zealand. Photo by Rowena Beaton.
FACING PAGE BOTTOM Paul Brennan at Wicklow Coast, Ireland.

WIDE CRACKS

Wide cracks can be divided into two categories, offwidths - cracks that are too wide to jam but too narrow to get inside - and chimneys - a crack that you can fit inside.

Wide crack climbing is an extremely creative form of climbing. The three dimensional nature of cracks and lack of conventional holds forces the climber to be inventive, improvising as they climb.

They are also incredibility strenuous and style goes out the window. Climbing a wide crack is like a no-holds-barred fight where you can use your elbows, knees, even your head.

OFFWIDTHS

Offwidths are by far the most difficult crack size and require a range of specialist techniques.

For narrow offwidths, hand stacking (*see facing page*) and jamming the knees work well. If the offwidth is wide enough to allow you to get your shoulder in, then arm bars and heel-toe jams are the way to go.

An arm bar is when you insert your inside arm, hand first, deep into the crack and create opposition by pressing the palm of your hand against one wall and your tricep/shoulder against the other.

A chicken wing is similar but the arm is bent and inserted into the crack elbow first. Chicken wings work well in narrow or flared constrictions.

CHIMNEYS

The classic chimney technique is known as 'back and foot' (*see top left*). It involves placing your back against one wall and the palms of your hands and feet (or sometimes knees) against the other. Height is gained, inch by inch, by moving first the hands then the feet .

Kneebars in cracks (see top left) are slightly different to those on face problems (see page 61). The sole of the foot is placed flat against the same side of the chimney as your back, while your knee presses into the opposite wall.

The major decision that needs to be made before you start up a chimney, is which direction to face. Very rarely would it be possible to change direction mid-way.

Wide chimneys can be bridged or in the most extreme cases climbed with hands on one wall and feet on the other, this is known as a full-body stem (*see top right*).

LEFT Dave Flanagan in Glendalough, Ireland. Photo by Trish Fox.
RIGHT Jamie Mullhall at Gravity, Dublin, Ireland.
FACING PAGE Paul Walters on Melvin Bragg , Ramshaw, UK. Photo by Simon Rawlinson.

5

DYNAMICS

When climbing bold traditional routes or soloing the climber must move in a very conservative, measured manner. However, the boulderer is free to experiment, using momentum to do moves that would be very difficult, if not impossible, in a more static style.

Of course all movement is by definition dynamic, but in climbing terminology a static move is one that is slow and balanced while a dynamic move is one that is done quickly, in one continuous motion.

Most of the techniques in this chapter require a fair amount of athletic ability, this suits some climbers more than others, however, dynamic movement can be learnt and refined with practise.

DEFINITIONS

The term dyno is often used to describe any dynamic move, but in this book it has a more specific meaning.

SLAP

A quick reach or lunge during which you have a minimum of two points of contact at all times.

JUMP

One hand stays on while both feet leave the rock so that you always have at least one point of contact.

DYNO

An all out leap during which the whole body is airborne and you, very briefly, have no points of contact (*see facing page*).

WHEN TO USE DYNAMICS?

Some climbers, usually those who have done a lot of trad climbing, move in a very static way while many younger climbers, who learnt to climb indoors, have a much looser, dynamic style.

Well executed dynamic movement is very

efficient. It requires less energy and power than static reaches, it's equivalent to pedalling down one hill so you can coast up the next.

Some problems are only possible by slapping, jumping or dynoing. However there are a few situations in which dynamic moves should be avoided:

- When facing a dangerous fall, the extra effort required to do a move statically is often justified by the control gained.

- When the target hold can only be held in a very precise manner, for example cracks, clusters of crystals, small pockets or narrow slots.

- On rough rock catching sharp holds at speed can be very hard on the skin.

SAFETY

Flinging yourself at the rock is dangerous, both because it can cause you to land awkwardly and because catching a hold at speed places a very high load on the fingers, arms, elbows and shoulders.

The best place to experiment with dynamics is at a quiet indoor wall with plenty of big holds and good matting.

It can be difficult to effectively spot a dynoing climber and there are times when the spotter is at greater risk of injury than the climber. Both spotter and climber need to use their judgement as each situation is different.

The potential landing zone for a big dyno is huge so think carefully about how and where you might land.

Remember to warm-up well (page 146) focussing on the shoulders and fingers. For long dynos it might be worth doing a few star jumps and stretches to prepare the big muscles in the legs.

PREVIOUS SPREAD Peter Kußler on Dr. Weed, Palatinate Forest, Germany. Photo by Rolf Seitz.
FACING PAGE Matt Wong on the Buckstone Dyno, Stanage, UK. Photo by Nic Mullin.

TRAJECTORY

An understanding of trajectory, the path taken by the centre of gravity, is particularly important for dynamic moves.

During a reach you accelerate initially before slowing down and stopping as you reach the target hold (the deadpoint). This means that gravity's effect becomes more pronounced in the later part of a move. On vertical rock gravity pulls you straight back down, but on overhanging rock it pulls you out (away from the rock) as well as down.

So depending on the circumstances your centre of gravity may travel in a curve (inward or outward), a figure of eight, a C shape (moving inward then outward) or a straight line (parallel or sometimes even perpendicular to the rock).

MEASURE UP

If the target hold is bad it might be worth hanging off it first, if you can get to it, to find the best way to hold it. This will also show you how far you have to travel from the foot holds.

Often the target is hard to see from below, marking it with a small dot of chalk can help but make sure you clean it off when you are finished. At the climbing wall a good way to gauge the length of a move is to count the bolt holes between holds (assuming the gaps are uniform).

HOLDING THE SWING

Sometimes reaching the target hold is relatively easy and holding the swing is the crux.

The greater the horizontal gap (out, across or both) between the launch foot holds and the target hand hold, the bigger the swing will be.

Depending on the situation you may reduce the swing by pulling your knees up towards your stomach or by arching your back towards the rock and allowing your lower legs

to swing outwards. Good core strength is key to holding the swing.

Use the momentum of the swing to get your feet back on the rock.

DEADPOINT

The deadpoint is the instant in a movement when your body is moving neither up nor down. It's the perfect time to grab a hold.

Every dynamic move should generate just enough momentum to reach the target hold and no more. With accurate use of momentum it's possible to make long reaches to very small holds.

CONFIDENCE

A lot of dynamics initially look and feel highly improbable, a few tentative attempts can help build confidence.

On very rough rock the best tactic is to get the distance dialled before committing to hanging the hold.

USE YOUR LEGS

The legs are the most powerful muscles in the body and should be the main should of the momentum required for big dynos and jumps. Think of your arms as a pivot and your legs as a spring.

FACING PAGE Jason Piper on Bitch Slap, Grampians, Australia. Photo by Tim Haasnoot.

GENERAL SEQUENCE

Dynamic moves require a blend of power and technique. As they take less than a second and involve the entire body working in harmony, they also require good coordination and lots of practice.

There are three phases to a dynamic movement: setup, launch and latch.

SETUP

The setup position is pretty similar for all dynamic moves.

The idea with sinking down before you launch is to maximise the amount of room available for generating momentum before you reach for the target.

Sometimes the best setup position may cause a huge swing once the target hold is latched, in that case you must launch from a sub-optimal position to increase the chances of holding the target hold.

There isn't any consensus on whether you should pump up and down a few times before launching. Some climbers believe that it gives a good feel for the best position, others think it's a waste of energy. Do whatever feels right to you.

- Choose the lowest foot holds that allow you to keep one or both feet on.

- Don't use two foot holds just for the sake of it, if they are very small or awkwardly positioned just use the best one.

- For long moves foot holds at staggered heights works best.

- The further the target the lower you should sink and the higher the foot holds need to be.

- Sink down by bending your legs and straightening your arms. Lock your eyes on the target.

LAUNCH

The idea behind the launch is to generate just enough momentum to carry you from one balanced position (setup) to another (latch), passing quickly through the unbalanced intermediate positions.

- Move upwards by simultaneously straightening the legs and pulling with the arms.

- The further the target, the faster you need to move, but remember that you want to stop moving just as the target hold comes into reach (the deadpoint).

- Move your hand(s) as late as possible. If possible leave one hand on and keep pushing down all the way through the movement.

LATCH

Often the crux is holding the target hold and controlling or preventing the swing. Big dynamic moves can be very hard on the skin, often failed attempts can do more damage than successful ones as the skin scrapes across the hold so once you hit the target commit 100% to holding it.

- If you judged the distance accurately you should reach the deadpoint just as the target hold comes into reach, this is the moment to grab it with a straight-ish arm.

- Prevent your feet from coming off the foot holds as your weight transfers to the target by pushing down hard on them.

- When jumping or dynoing, your feet will be in the air and may well swing hard once you latch the target.

FACING PAGE Jorge Crespo, Dyno, Albarracín, Spain. Photo by Jorge Crespo.

SLAP

A slap is just a quick reach or lunge during which one hand and (at least) one foot is always in contact with the rock.

Slapping has two major advantages over reaching statically. Firstly, a lot of moves are significantly easier if done dynamically and secondly it's often more efficient ie. it's quicker and uses less energy. Slapping is an essential skill for every boulderer.

Sloping holds can't resist an outward pull so they are particularly difficult to reach from, the lower your centre of gravity relative to the sloper the more positive they feel. Slapping initiates the movement from a low position and uses it to carry you to the target.

When the target hold is small or narrow (for example a pocket) it's easy to fumble or miss it entirely. Work on your accuracy by slapping to narrow sloping holds (make sure your fingers are well warmed up first) but avoid dynamic moves to small pockets as it's a common cause of finger injuries.

1

Setup with one high foot hold and sink down by straightening the arms. The higher your feet the further you can reach without cutting loose, but if they are too high it can be awkward to generate momentum.

2

Initiate the launch by pulling in and down with your arms. The idea is to straighten your higher leg rather than push off it, you want to keep your foot on. If you have staggered feet the lower one may come off.

On short moves, especially on steep rock, pulling your chest towards the rock can be enough to allow you reach the target.

At the last possible moment move your hand, making sure that your lower hand keeps pulling and that the wrist is as low as possible to maintain a downward pull.

3

On hard slaps when the holds are very small it's vital to keep at least one foot on, in fact doing so is often the crux. Your foot is most likely to come off as your weight transfers onto the target hold. Concentrate on pulling/pushing with every point of contact as you latch the target.

ABOVE Dave Flanagan in Bullock Harbour, Ireland.

JUMP

A jump is a dynamic move in which both feet leave the rock but one hand stays on. Jumping is necessary when you are faced with a long reach to the next hand hold and no high foot holds. Keeping one hand on allows smaller target holds to be held.

On very steep rock (> 45° overhanging) jumping is often a better option than slapping from poor foot holds, as you have more control over the inevitable swing.

If you are jumping from very positive hand holds you can generate more momentum by dangling one hand down by your side and swinging it upwards as you launch.

A jump start (see page 100) is a jump done from the ground to the first holds of a problem.

1

As the foot holds are low and the hand holds high, there isn't much room to sink down.

2

Spring hard off the foot holds. Reach with your lower hand and use your higher hand to guide you towards the target.

On vertical rock you need to bend your higher arm as your body rises to keep your centre of gravity close to the rock, but on steeper ground keep it straight to take advantage of the pivot effect.

3

As jumps are most common on steep ground, your body will usually swing outwards once you catch the target hold. Minimise this swing by trying to get your centre of gravity as directly below the target hold as possible, this means jumping up and outwards rather than just straight up.

Jumps are prone to a particular type of cut loose in which the body rotates one way and then the other. This twisting motion is very difficult to resist, a strong core is required.

1

2

DYNO

A dyno is an all out leap during which, for a brief glorious moment, you are fully airborne. Outdoors true (non-eliminate) dynos are rare and much prized.

Really long dynos (more than 2m between hand holds) often require a stepping motion (*see left*). This involves pushing off the hand holds (or another high foot hold) with your foot to get extra height. Needless to say this requires serious spring and coordination.

1

Pumping up and down a few times before takeoff gives a sense of the move without committing, but it's probably not necessary after the first few attempts.

The position of the foot holds is more important than their size. Ideally they should be staggered, with one higher than the other. Put your stronger leg on the higher one to provide the 'kick', while the lower foot provides the initial thrust.

For sideways dynos place the foot closest to the target on the higher hold.

2

Spring hard off the foot holds and push down hard with both hands.

3

The target hold is usually caught with one hand, but using two hands (a double dyno) makes sticking marginal holds or holding big swings easier. Even when the target is initially latched with one hand it's best to match it as quickly as possible.

LEFT Peter McMahon on Rainbow Rocket, Fontainebleau, France.

OTHER TECHNIQUES

The following dynamic techniques are very useful and are rarely encountered in other forms of climbing.

JUMP STARTS

Steep, difficult or blank starts can be overcome by jumping from the ground to the first good holds, this technique is known as a jump start (AKA French start).

Jump starts come in three variations: a jump from the ground (*see above*), a jump assisted by a hand hold and a step using a foot hold to reach the target (*see right*).

The key to any dynamic start is launching from the point on the ground that will minimise the swing when you latch the target. It can take a bit of experimenting to find this point.

Generate extra momentum by swinging your free arm(s) upwards as you jump.

Catch the hold with both hands if possible. Jumping to two separate holds requires good coordination but if neither hold is sufficient on its own you have no choice.

ABOVE Dave Flanagan on Greg's Problem, Glendalough, Ireland.
RIGHT Dave Flanagan in Wicklow, Ireland. Photo by Simon McGovern.

RUN AND JUMP

Some problems with blank starts, that might otherwise be impossible, can be solved using a run and jump (*see above*). As the name suggests you run at the rock, kick off one or more foot holds and jump for the hand holds. Probably more parkour than climbing but very satisfying when it works out.

CAMPUSING

Campusing is climbing without using your feet and unless you are very strong it has to be dynamic (*see left*). Steep rock is tiring and sometimes it's more efficient to campus rather than waste energy struggling with marginal foot holds.

Campusing should be done at speed, carrying momentum from one move into the next, like swinging across the monkey bars in the playground.

Kicking your legs (known as kipping) as you move can add an extra few inches to your reach.

ABOVE Toby Wright on Lateral Mindset, Saint Bees, UK. Photo by Peter Wilkinson.
LEFT Al Sarhan, Aughris Head, Ireland. Photo by Jeff Gardner.

6

INDOORS

Indoor climbing walls have been the main driver of bouldering's recent surge in popularity. They are a friendly, comfortable environment in which to introduce beginners to climbing, a social hub and a place to train during cold, wet, dark winters.

Not only have walls helped boulderers to get stronger but they have also influenced the type of problems climbers seek when (or if) they boulder outdoors.

Some indoor climbers see their local wall as a gym of sorts, a place to get fit and socialise. Their interest and knowledge of climbing doesn't extend beyond it's walls. This attitude may seem strange to climbers with a more traditional outlook, but it's going to become increasingly common.

The onus is on experienced climbers to steer beginners in the right direction, sharing their knowledge of climbing tradition, history, ethics and etiquette.

SAFETY

In climbing terms indoor walls are as safe as it gets, but there are a few thing to bear in mind:

- Warm-up well. It's tempting to jump straight onto the harder problems but building up gradually reduces the changes of injury and you will climb better for longer. See page 146 for information about warming up.

- Watch out for people beneath you as you climb and be aware of other climbers when walking around. Don't sit or lie about on the mats.

- At modern walls the matting is generally excellent but watch out for gaps, edges or soft spots.

INDOOR STYLE

Route setters, wall builders and hold manufactures are continually creating new challenges for climbers that, while attempting to mimic climbing on rock, are also unique and interesting climbs in themselves.

If a problem feels much harder than the grade suggests, you are probably missing something. Compared to problems outdoors there are limited options in terms of holds and hence fewer opportunities to make good movement or problem solving skills count.

Route setters use volumes (*see next page*) to make the climbing more three dimensional. Volumes are large plywood shapes (usually triangular or rounded), massive holds upon which other holds can be mounted. Used intelligently, volumes make for quasi-outdoor style problems that are very powerful but at the same time technical.

FEATURED WALLS

Featured walls (*see facing page*) have a rock-like surface which is supplemented with bolt on holds. The texture is similar to polished rock that is covered in edges and smears, on some walls it's possible to climb using these features alone.

Problems on featured walls feel more natural than those on flat plywood panels as there is a large variety of realistic holds. However, once you are familiar with the specific features they can all start to feel a little similar.

CIRCUITS

A circuit is a collection of problems of similar difficulty. They usually feature a wide range of styles so they are a good test of all round ability and a useful way to gauge your strengths and weaknesses. Climbing a long circuit in a single session is a very enjoyable way to build endurance for long days and trips.

The term circuit is also used to describe very long problems that are used to train endurance for routes.

PREVIOUS SPREAD Rustam Gelmanov competing in the Go-Pro Games in Vail, Colorado, US. Photo by Brent La Fleur.
FACING PAGE David Mason in The Foundry, Sheffield, UK. Photo by Paul Bennett.

COMPETITIONS

Competitions are a regular feature at most walls but unless you are competing at an elite level they are usually quite informal.

The format typically consists of a number of problems of various grades and a set time in which to attempt them. You may have a fixed number of attempts with ascents earning points on a sliding scale or there may be unlimited tries, in which case each ascent is worth the same, irrespective of how many attempts required.

A good warm-up is vital to perform well at a competition. If there is a section of wall to warm-up on make the most of it, otherwise, start with the easiest problems and gradually increase the difficulty.

At smaller walls or busy competitions the area beneath problems can get dangerously crowded, so make sure that there is sufficient landing space before you start each problem. When you aren't climbing watch where you stand.

TRAINING

Climbing walls opened up the world of physical training to the climber. They are the biggest factor in the recent increases in climbing standards.

Training on indoor walls is discussed in detail on page 151.

READING PROBLEMS

Most walls mark problems by the colour of the holds or using tags.

Here is a suggested approach to reading (figuring out how to climb) indoor problems.

- Identify the start and finish holds. Is it a sitting, standing or jump start?
- Locate the rest of the holds, making sure you don't miss any around corners, under roofs etc. Are you 'allowed' to use volumes or permanent features?

- Is there an obvious crux ie. a section with long reaches or bad holds?
- Examine the starting move, what hand should go where for it? Simulate these hands through the rest of the problem, does it work?
- If it doesn't work, do you need to match, cross through, do two consecutive moves with the same hand or completely re-think the sequence?
- Once you have a hand sequence, figure out the foot sequence and then integrate them.
- Holds that have only been used by the feet will be unchalked and there may be rubber marks on the wall surrounding them.
- On longer problems look out for any places where you can get a rests using a kneebar, bridging, heel hook etc.
- Watch out for red herrings, holds that aren't essential to the sequence, which have been added by the route setter to distract and confuse.
- Have a plan B in case your original sequence doesn't work.

Of course you could just watch others or ask for advice, but that won't do anything for your problem-reading skills.

FACING PAGE Sierra Blair Coyle competing in the Seattle Bouldering Challenge, US. Photo by Dirk Houghton.

7

OUTDOORS

Bouldering outdoors is a very different from bouldering at the wall and this can come as a shock to some beginners.

Be prepared to struggle on your first few visits outdoors, it isn't realistic to expect to immediately be able to climb at the same standard as you do indoors.

Discover outdoor bouldering on your own terms, climb whatever you like the look of and don't worry whether it's an 'established' problem or not.

LANDINGS

The combination of less than perfect landings and insecure moves can be very intimidating for an inexperienced boulderer. Start out on easy, low problems and gradually build up to the harder, higher ones. See page 27 for information about spotting, matting and falling.

EQUIPMENT

Bouldering outdoors requires some extra equipment, primarily a bouldering pad (see page 24 for more information).

SKIN

The first few times you boulder on rough rock your skin will take a beating. There's no way around this but your skin will soon toughen up if you climb outside regularly.

CONDITIONS

Don't underestimate the difference that good conditions can make. The friction on cold, dry days is significantly better than on warm, humid days and this can make bouldering, especially on friction dependant problems, feel a lot easier. Friction is discussed in more detail on page 118.

To get the most out of your day's bouldering let the weather influence your choice of destination. If conditions are bad, it may well be more profitable in the long term to set aside your goals and just have a fun day's climbing rather than getting demoralised struggling on hard problems.

PREVIOUS SPREAD John Watson, Caisteal Abhail, Arran, Scotland. Photo by John Watson.
ABOVE Seamus O'Boyle and Ieuan Rickard on The Rosetta Stone, Arran, Scotland. Photo by Christine Ratcliffe.

COLD

The best friction is found on cold, dry days. Climbing in the cold is an integral part of outdoor bouldering, it's the reason why boulderers are associated with woolly hats and down jackets.

A good warm-up is vital, especially in the cold. A brisk walk followed by a few easy problems will get the blood flowing. As you get warmer shed layers, but remember to put them back on while resting between attempts.

A hot drink, gloves and leggings under your trousers can all help on really cold days. If you have poor circulation, a chemical hand warmer can be useful for defrosting your fingers or toes.

When the temperature gets close to 0°C (32°F) anything stronger than a gentle breeze feels arctic so stick to sheltered areas.

HOT

Bouldering in hot, humid conditions is very tiring and the diminished friction can be frustrating. Make the best of the conditions by:

- Seeking out problems that are shaded and exposed to any breeze.
- Climbing early in the morning or late in the evening when it's cooler.
- Focus on steep problems with big holds. They won't be as badly effected by the lack of friction as those with small or sloping holds.

When applying sun cream or insect repellent avoid getting it on the fingertips as it's very greasy, but if you do, liquid chalk is the best way to remove any residue.

WET

Overhanging problems that face away from the wind may stay dry in a shower but only the steepest rock will stay dry in heavy or prolonged rain. Ask around to find out which areas are best in wet weather as local knowledge is vital.

Clean rock dries quickly in a strong wind so if you are caught out by a passing shower it's often worth sheltering and waiting for the rock to dry.

Some forms of sandstone are very brittle when wet so should be avoided on damp days otherwise you risk breaking holds.

ABOVE John Palmer in the Bronx Cave, New Zealand. Photo by Tom Hoyle.

ANIMALS

Anyone spending time outdoors should be prepared for pests and, in some parts of the world, predators.

Midge are tiny (1-4mm) flying insects which are most common in temperate climates during the summer months on humid, still days. Insect repellent and a fine mesh head-net help, but the best strategy is to avoid sheltered areas near water and vegetation especially around dusk.

Ticks, tiny insects that carry Lyme Disease, can also be an issue if you are walking through thick undergrowth.

In tropical climates mosquitoes can be a problem, they are less annoying than midge but are more dangerous as they can transmit disease.

In areas where there are snakes or bears you should get specialist advice about what precautions to take.

STANDARDS

Bouldering is an activity without any formal rules or regulations, but there is one maxim all climbers agree on - never damage the rock. More specifically:

- Never chip or alter holds in any way. If you can't climb a problem as it stands train harder or leave it for someone better.

- Never use a wire brush to clean holds, a stiff plastic bristled brush is sufficient.

- Avoid excessive damage of vegetation when cleaning new problems. See page 121 for advice on cleaning.

- Pof, a dried pine resin that increases friction, is used by a minority of climbers in Fontainebleau, but pof should never be used outside of Fontainebleau, as it polishes the rock, making the holds very slippery.

- Make sure your shoes are clean and dry. Dirty shoes erode the rock significantly faster than clean ones.

ABOVE Eddie Gianelloni on the Eriksson Problem, Horse Flats, California, US. Photo by Eddie Gianelloni.

As well as looking after the rock remember to show some consideration for your fellow climbers.

- Keep noise to a minimum and leave your speakers at home.
- If a problem is busy wait your turn or return later. Don't monopolise a problem, welcome others to try it alongside you.
- Don't litter and if you see any pick it up.
- Keep in mind that some climbers are keen to hear beta while others prefer to work it out for themselves.

ETHICS

Thankfully bouldering is largely free of the ethical dilemmas that exist in other climbing genres, you either climb a problem or you don't.

Sometimes highballs are practised on a top rope before being climbed rope-less (known as 'headpointing' in trad climbing). Obviously it's better style to do a problem without top-roping first ('ground up') but it's an entirely personal choice.

CHALK

Keep chalk use to a minimum, excessive chalk is unsightly and entirely counter productive. Remember non-climbers may consider your chalk marks as graffiti.

If you must mark a hard to see hold, make the tick as small as possible - a thumbprint should suffice and don't forget to brush it off when you are finished.

Never put chalk on foot holds or your shoes, it's pointless, chalk isn't glue, all it does is absorb sweat.

If you anticipate getting into a position where you will be unable to reach into your chalk bag, but need chalk, rub plenty of chalk into your trouser leg or sleeve. A quick pat will re-coat your hands.

Some brands of chalk contain a drying agent that, if left on the skin, can dry it out and make it brittle so wash it off your hands as soon as possible after climbing.

ABOVE Michal Madera on The Shoreditch Park Boulder, London, UK. Photo by Michal Madera.

Whipping holds with the tail end of a cloth is a great way to remove loose chalk and dust from holds.

GETTING DOWN

Most boulders have straightforward descents, but there are exceptions so It's worth doing a quick reconnaissance of the downclimb. While you are up there you can check out the top out.

There are situations when it's better to jump off in control rather than attempt a sketchy downclimb, either way get someone to place a few pads beneath you.

SIT STARTS

To the non-climber nothing exemplifies the pointlessness of bouldering more than the sit start and even the most devoted boulderer can't deny how convoluted they are. Having said that, sitting starts have their place.

- A low start extracts the maximum amount of climbing from the rock.

- Very difficult or contorted moves can be tried in safety when you are inches rather than feet above the ground.

- The difficulty of some problems is very dependant on how high you can reach from the ground, in this case a low start on a defined hold can level the playing field.

MOUNTAIN BOULDERING

Getting off the beaten track and exploring and bouldering high in the hills is one of the most satisfying bouldering experiences.

The longer days, dry ground and relatively cool temperatures of summer make the mountains a great place to boulder in the warmer months of the year.

If the landings are bad the best solution is to round up a group of boulderers so you have plenty of pads and spotters. Don't be tempted to stash your pad at the boulders to save carrying it, as this could be considered littering and may be frowned upon by the land owners.

When visiting remote areas make sure you are equipped for a long day out. Pack both warm and waterproof layers, food and drink and wear suitable shoes.

COASTAL BOULDERING

Coastal bouldering is a great option for climbers who haven't much experience outdoors. The rock is usually easy on the hands, the climbing is more physical than technical and the landings are usually good.

Conditions at areas exposed to the sea can be very fickle and difficult to predict due to humidity, tides, seepage and spray. However, the weather is usually drier and warmer near the coast.

Any rock that is regularly battered by the sea will be solid, but watch out for rock that is out of reach of the waves as it can be loose. Downclimb or jump off rather than risk a dangerous top out on questionable rock.

Climbing close to the sea has its dangers. Keep an eye on the tide in case your exit route gets cut off and watch our for large swells that come out of nowhere and sweep across ledges washing everything in their path out to sea.

Sand and climbing shoes don't mix, a tarp - to spread on the ground - and a towel - to clean your shoes - are useful.

Misguided climbers have in the past, used blowtorches to dry damp holds, this is a very bad idea as heated rock expands potentially breaking holds.

FACING PAGE Lexi Tuddenham, Paradox Valley, Colorado, US. Photo by Christian Prellwitz.

GRADES

A problem's grade is an indication of how difficult it is to climb assuming good conditions and the best sequence. The grade doesn't take into account the height of the problem or the difficulty of figuring out how to do it.

Difficulty in climbing is highly subjective and is dependant on many factors (body type, height, experience, conditions etc). To account for all these factors and accurately express that difficulty in a simple grading system is almost impossible. So don't take grades too seriously, treat them as rough guesses and a crude means of identifying suitable problems. Don't make the mistake of equating difficulty and grade, remember 'the map is not the territory'.

There are two bouldering grading systems in use internationally:

- The Font system, which originated in Fontainebleau near Paris almost a century ago. Font is unique in that problems are assembled into circuits (groups of problems of similar difficulty). These circuits are marked by arrows and numbers with the colour corresponding to the difficulty of the circuit (*see above*).

- The V or Hueco system which was invented by John Sherman to grade problems in Hueco Tanks, Texas in the early nineties.

Both systems have their pros and cons, but as they correspond closely it's largely academic which is used.

The table on page 190 shows the two systems and gives a very approximate indication of how they compare with route grades at the lower end.

GUIDEBOOKS

At most indoor walls the problems are marked using colour coding or tags and the start and finish holds clearly defined. Outdoors it's a different story, if you are lucky there will be a guidebook or a fellow boulderer might point out a few problems.

Guidebooks use two methods to describe problems, simple maps (*see right*) or photos of the rock with the line taken by the problems superimposed (*see above*). Some guides give detailed descriptions of the starting and finishing positions and the moves in between, while others just briefly describe the line ("Climb the arete on its left hand side").

In some bouldering areas you may encounter eliminates which are problems with specific rules that dictate what holds may and may not be used. They are a way of getting the most climbing out of a limited amount of rock.

There is no point worrying about whether you are climbing the 'right' problems, just use your common sense and try whatever looks interesting.

The Ruins

FRICTION

Bouldering in good conditions is equivalent to cycling with the wind at your back.

Understanding friction, knowing what constitutes good conditions and taking advantage of them can make the difference between success and failure.

CONTACT AREA

In theory, friction is independent of the size of the contact area but this rule doesn't hold in climbing situations. The more rubber or skin in contact with the rock the better.

HANDS

The skin on our hands can only resist a certain amount of pressure before it tears. Increasing the contact area between our hands and the rock is vital, as not only does this increase the grip, but it also reduces pressure and thus the chances of damaging the skin.

CHALK

Chalk creates a slippery granular layer that reduces friction, but for the vast majority of climbers it's essential as the sweat from our hands reduces friction more than chalk does. Excess chalk has a detrimental effect on grip, so blow the excess off your hands before you start climbing and if conditions are good, only use a small amount.

FEET

Climbing shoe rubber works primarily by deforming and moulding to the rock. Rubber's hardness and hence grip varies with temperature. At low temperatures rubber is harder and doesn't mould well to the rock while at higher temperatures it deforms too easily and slips.

Manufacturers design their shoes' rubber to perform optimally at a specific temperature (approximately 5°C). This temperature is chosen as any colder is too uncomfortable to climb and any warmer and the hands may sweat. Hard rubber that won't deform and roll is ideal for small edges, but when smearing a relatively soft rubber that will mould to the rock is better.

ROCK

It's obvious that a rough rock like granite will have more friction than a smooth rock like slate, but what about sandstone which isn't as rough as granite but has a similar level of grip?

Once rock reaches a certain roughness the irregularities become so large that rubber or skin can't mould to them. After this point increasing roughness causes decreasing friction.

WEATHER

Temperature, wind and humidity all affect friction.

At low temperatures our hands sweat less and our skin becomes harder (the cold reduces the fluidity of the liquids that constitute our cellular membranes). This is good up to the point when our hands become too numb to climb.

A strong wind can give good conditions on warm summer days or make cold winter days unbearable.

In high humidity, the rate of evaporation of sweat from the skin decreases. High humidity can also cause problems with condensation and dew on the rock itself.

ROCK TYPES

It's only natural for climbers to take an interest in the rock they dedicate so much time to climbing on.

It isn't that easy to generalise about the different rock types from a climbing point of view as environmental and geological factors can have a huge effect on a rock's characteristics. For example, granite is usually

very rough, but granite that's close to the sea can be worn to a marble-like finish.

To be suitable for bouldering, rock needs to be pretty solid, relatively clean (or cleanable) and neither too featured nor too blank. Everything else is just a matter of taste.

LIMESTONE

Broadly speaking limestone can be either quite featured with lots of small edges and pockets or it can be very smooth and rounded. Either way the friction is low.

Limestone can also form tufas and stalactites. Tufas are snake like features, that are usually pinched. Stalactites are free hanging spikes found in roofs.

While friendly on the skin, small crimps and pockets can be hard on the tendons and ligaments of the fingers, so warm the fingers up very well.

GRANITE

Granite is one of the roughest rock types commonly bouldered on. Most problems rely on friction, which means slopers for the hands and smearing for the feet.

Some types of granite contain a lot of quartz crystals, that can be used as tiny hand or foot holds.

A lot of granite boulders are erratics, boulders that have been left behind by a receding glacier. These heavily eroded boulders tend to be round and relatively featureless.

SANDSTONE AND GRITSTONE

Sandstone is considered by many as the best rock to boulder on. While not as rough, or as hard on the hands as granite, the fine grain still offers excellent friction.

In Fontainebleau the sandstone, particularly on the rounded tops of boulders forms a distinctive elephant hide texture (*see above*). There are a massive range of hold types, but the characteristic sandstone hold is the sloper. You are also likely to come across lots of tiny crimps known as grattons in Font.

Gritstone is a specific form of sandstone, that is abundant in the north of England. Grit is less featured than other forms of sandstone and the holds tend to be very rounded, this makes conditions absolutely critical to success.

Pebbles, which are common on grit, are tiny stones protruding from the surface, they are usually very small accommodating one finger at most.

OTHER

There are many other rock types that are either less common or less popular for climbing including slate, rhyolite, gneiss, basalt, dolerite, gabbro, conglomerate and schist.

ABOVE The unique texture of Fontainebleau sandstone. Photo by Ciaran Mulhall.

FIRST ASCENTS

The process of finding, cleaning, climbing and documenting new problems is one of the most interesting aspects of bouldering.

Even in Fontainebleau, the largest and oldest bouldering area in the world, there are new problems of all grades waiting to be climbed.

The lure of a first ascent is a great motivator and can awaken competitive instincts, driving you to climb harder than ever before.

Sharing information and documenting new problems and areas is vital, but it probably isn't necessary to exhaustively catalogue every single problem and variation, some things are best discovered for oneself (or not at all).

LANDINGS

Sometimes it's possible to improve a bad landing by shifting a few rocks or placing some branches across a hole. However, serious modification of the landing zone, especially of an established problem, may cause trouble with other climbers or the landowners. Never do anything that could threaten access, consult other climbers and think carefully before you act.

CLAIMING

While no one is obliged to report their first ascents, if you say nothing you can't really complain if someone claims 'your' problem.

Some climbers who are lucky enough to find new areas, do the lion's share of the problems before spreading the word, which is reasonable.

Hoarding of areas and problems is unfair and it would be a shame for climbing to become like surfing with its 'secret spots' and 'locals only' attitude.

LOOSE ROCK

At some coastal areas the rock above the high tide mark, out of reach of the sea, can be significantly looser than the lower rock. In that case, it's probably safer to remove loose holds before you climb rather than risk them giving way suddenly when you pull on them.

However, there is a fine line between creating and cleaning holds. Gluing loose holds is a bad idea, if a hold falls off a problem, just leave it.

EQUIPMENT

Some of the following equipment might be useful for cleaning new problems:

- Brushes, the more the better as they tend to clog with dirt. A range of sizes, large ones for slopers and small narrow ones for thin cracks and awkward corners. Washing up brushes work well.

- For large expanses of dirty rock a yard brush will save time.

- A telescopic pole that brushes can be attached to is very handy. Taping a brush to a walking pole or stick works well.

- A small saw and secateurs can be useful for trimming vegetation. Think long and hard before cutting down a tree.

- A shovel for levelling landings.

- Sometimes the only way to be able to get at the holds is by abseiling. Use a self locking device or a prusik so that you can work safely with both hands.

- A short lightweight ladder can be more convenient than abseiling if you don't have far to carry it.

CLEANING

Cleaning new problems can involve serious work, cutting branches, peeling back moss and scrubbing the rock. Before you start, ask yourself is the problem going to justify the effort and is the cleaning going to cause any access issues?

Here are a few things to bear in mind when cleaning problems:

- Try the moves a few times before you start brushing to determine what needs cleaning and what doesn't and then only remove what's necessary.
- Never use a wire brush.
- A heavy canvas cloth is excellent for cleaning rock with a loose grain.
- Clean from the top down otherwise you will just be brushing dirt onto clean holds.
- Remember to clean just above and below hand holds as this is where you thumb or palm may be.

The most important thing to remember is that under no circumstances chip or alter the rock in any way.

LEFT Dec Tormey cleaning holds in Poll Na Péist, Galway, Ireland.

HIGHBALLS

Tall problems are known as highballs. There is no universal definition of how high is high and it really comes down to an individual's ability and tolerance for risk. One man's easy warm-up is another man's brush with death.

The difference between a highball and a short route is just as subjective and it depends as much on the style that it's done in (bouldering pads, top-rope practice) as the height.

Highballing is, to a large extent, a mind game. Moves that feel easy a few inches above the ground are an entirely different matter twenty feet up.

PREPARE

Before you commit to a highball think about the consequences of a fall. Will it be a long but safe drop onto the pads? Is there a chance of injury? At what point does it become inadvisable to fall?

Checking the holds is best practice for normal problems, but for highballs it's essential.

Grades are rarely accurate and being scared and pumped isn't conducive to figuring out the optimal sequence, so leave a large margin if you don't want to risk falling.

ROPE

Top roping is an option if there is a highball you really want to do but can't justify the risk. Some climbers figure out and rehearse the moves on a top rope before soloing it (this is known as headpointing). Headpointing allows you to do much harder routes/highballs than you could do in a ground-up style.

Whether you top rope or not is a personal choice, a matter of style that has no bearing on anyone else.

BAD LANDINGS

Some boulderers also define problems with bad landings as highballs, this is sensible as they both require similar tactics and mind-set. Obviously the more pads the better, but don't let them lull you into a false sense of security, it's very hard to predict where and how you will land.

CONTROL

If you feel there is a reasonable chance of injury then you must climb in a conservative style, similar to how you would solo a route rather than climb a conventional boulder problem. Often it's prudent to choose a harder but more static solution over an easier dynamic one, the greater control justifies the extra effort.

The best tactic for highballs is to climb up and down, going a little higher each time, coming down to rest and gather your thoughts until you feel ready to commit.

STAMINA

An extra few feet of climbing, combined with the inevitable over-gripping of holds can make highballing much more demanding of stamina than normal bouldering.

WHY HIGHBALL?

Highballing isn't for everyone, some boulderers feel that taking risks and having to climb very conservatively is counter to the whole spirit of bouldering. But to others, especially those with a background in trad climbing, risk taking is an essential part of the climbing experience and some of the best problems in the world are highballs.

FACING PAGE Mina Leslie-Wujastyk on Midnight Lightning, Yosemite, California, US. Photo by David Mason.

OTHER CLIMBING

Bouldering is only one of the many distinct, but related, forms of rock climbing.

ALPINE CLIMBING

Alpine climbing is climbing mountains and it's at the opposite end of the spectrum to bouldering. Alpine routes can be long multi-pitch rock routes or they can involve snow and ice climbing.

TRADITIONAL CLIMBING

Traditional ('trad') climbing is climbing routes protected with gear placed by the leader. A lot of boulderers find the moves on trad routes relatively easy but struggle with the exposure/fear element.

The best way to become a safe, competent trad climber is to find an experienced climber who is willing to take you under their wing and start on very easy routes before gradually increasing the difficulty as your skills and confidence improve.

SPORT CLIMBING

Sport climbing is climbing routes that are protected by in situ bolts and in theory it's safer than trad climbing. Sport routes tend to be steep and sustained which can cause problems for boulderers who lack stamina.

SOLOING

Soloing is climbing routes without a rope. A lot of climbers have done some soloing but they usually stay deep inside their comfort zone.

Soloing requires a lot of experience, a cool head, self confidence and a very solid, controlled climbing style. Needless to say it's extremely dangerous and not for beginners.

HIGHBALLING

The line between soloing and climbing high boulder problems, known as highballs, can be fine and really is down to individual's risk tolerance and skills. For more about highballing see page 122.

BUILDERING

Buildering is climbing on buildings or other man-made structures. It's the last resort of the rock starved and popular with climbers on their way home from the pub.

DEEP WATER SOLOING

Climbing above water without a rope is known as deep water soloing (*see facing page*). It has become popular in recent years, but it can be dangerous. You must be a strong swimmer, and always check the depth of the water. Make sure that you will be able to get out of the water before you start to climb.

NIGHT BOULDERING

Bouldering in the dark is a good option in the depths of winter when you are sick of the wall. During the summer do it to take advantage of the cooler conditions at night.

Everything feels harder and scarier in the dark, even problems you know well feel completely different. At a minimum you need a good head torch, but a couple of gas lamps or lanterns make a big difference.

COMPETITION CLIMBING

Indoor competition climbing is now a professional sport and many athletes focus entirely on lead or bouldering competitions, training hard and rarely climbing on rock.

FACING PAGE Ewan Sinclair on Seaward Arete, Baring Head, New Zealand. Photo by Tom Hoyle.

8

STRATEGY

Bouldering strategy is all about making the best use of your time and energy.

Experienced climbers make good strategic choices, they choose suitable goals, they know how long to rest, they know when to call it a day and when to have just one more go. This chapter is about the logic underlying these decisions.

As with every other aspect of climbing, the best way to learn about strategy and become one of those boulderers who gets things done, is by making mistakes and learning from them.

PREPARATION

A little preparation can stack the odds in your favour.

GOALS

Goals are an excellent source of motivation and without them it's impossible to train effectively.

The most obvious goal in bouldering is to climb a specific problem, but other goals could include completing a group (or circuit) of problems, re-climbing problems you have done before, training related (do X pull ups) or to doing a specific move or link on a project.

Of course, there are times when you should just enjoy a fun and relaxing day without worrying about grades or goals.

TRIPS

There is nothing quite like visiting a world-class bouldering area (see some suggestions on page 161) and completely immersing yourself in bouldering for a few days.

Strategy is critical on trips, when time is limited and failing on a problem may mean having to wait a long time for another opportunity to try it.

A trip is a great source of motivation for training. Do some research, maybe draw up a 'tick-list' and train on similar holds and features at home.

To get the most out of a short trip you need to climb a few days in a row before taking a rest day. This is hard on the body, so prepare by climbing as much as possible including climbing multiple days in a row. You daily sessions don't need to be very long, even just doing a few easy problems will stand to you.

It's easy in the excitement of visiting a new area to get carried away, but remember to pace yourself. Don't overdo it on the first day, spend some time on easy problems to get accustomed to the rock.

Once the skin on your fingertips becomes very thin or sore it takes days to heal, so you are better off not letting it get too bad in the first place.

BETA

Beta is information about the best (ie. easiest) way to climb a problem. Obviously it's highly subjective, a six and half foot male will climb most problems very differently from a four foot teenager.

Most climbers are happy to share advice and tips, but don't fall in the trap of only trying a problem the way you are told or shown. Awareness of your strengths and weaknesses will help you adapt other climber's sequences. Never be afraid to reject other people's beta and experiment with alternative sequences.

Remember some climbers like the challenge of solving problems for themselves, so ask before giving away all of a problem's tricks.

THE MIND

The mental aspects of bouldering performance are overlooked by a lot of climbers, there is a tendency to focus on strength and power. This is a missed opportunity as bouldering, in particular sieging long-term projects and highballing, requires considerable mental fortitude.

Success on a hard problem only comes after a lot of effort and many failed attempts, so learning to cope with failure is an essential part of bouldering.

Bouldering isn't dangerous but at times fear can be a factor, planting a seed of doubt in the mind, causing hesitation and a reluctance to commit.

And while it's quite rational to be concerned about a hard move 25 feet above a bad landing, it's another thing when you are only a foot or two above your pad.

Rather than try and ignore these feelings it can be better to address them and put yourself at ease. Once you are satisfied that what you are about to do is safe, you are free to commit 100%. However, if you can't commit, or still have reservations, it might be best to move on to another problem.

There is another type of fear that is probably more relevant to bouldering - the fear of failing or looking bad. Some climbers are afraid to be seen failing or can't perform in front of a crowd. This can be very limiting, as without pushing ourselves and falling off sometimes, it's almost impossible to improve.

When linking together steep, physical problems, an aggressive approach can be effective, but a calmer, considered approach is usually best on more delicate, technical problems or when trying to figure out the moves. Some climbers find that shouting or grunting can get them through powerful moves, which is fair enough, but bear in mind it can be a little annoying for those nearby.

If your are lucky you may experience days

when you are able to completely focus on your climbing and it feels effortless. This is the psychological state of flow (or being 'in the zone'). And while this feeling can't be conjured up at will, studies show that three preconditions must be met to achieve a state of flow:

• There must be a clear set of goals (getting to the top of a problem).

• The task must have clear and immediate feedback (falling off).

• A good balance between the perceived challenges of the task and your perceived skills. You must be confident that you are capable of the task. Easy problems probably won't be engaging enough, and problems that are far too hard will only frustrate. So the key is to find problems that are just within your grasp.

Visualisation is a powerful technique that is particularly useful for long or complicated sequences. By working through the moves in your head before you attempt a problem, you refresh them in your mind so that you can move quickly and decisively once you pull onto the rock. Detailed visualisation can also reveal if there are any parts of the sequence that you are unsure of before you pull onto the rock.

While bouldering is excellent at focussing the mind, sometimes that focus can be on the wrong thing, for example worrying about whether your spotter is paying attention, when you should be focussing on placing your foot.

Working a hard problem requires a positive attitude, as the final goal - climbing the problem - is often distant. Look for other milestones that can be used to measure progress and keep your motivation high.

TACTICS

Tactics are the little details that can be the difference between success and failure.

FLASH

To flash a problem is to climb it on the first attempt. You can get beta, feel the holds and watch others try it, once you climb it from start to finish on your first attempt.

Flashing a problem is very satisfying whether it's a skin of the teeth battle or a very controlled cruise.

It can be worth putting effort into flashing problems, especially steep, indoor-style ones. However, on long problems where stamina is a factor it makes more sense to conserve your energy and work the problem in sections before trying it from the start.

BREATHE

Many physical activities that have similarities with climbing, such as martial arts, yoga and weight lifting, place huge emphasis on coordinating breathing and movement. Breathing correctly maximises oxygen flow to your muscles, helps you relax and improves focus.

However a lot of boulderers neglect their breathing while climbing. Advanced breathing techniques are outside the scope of this book. Just remember to take a few deep breaths before you pull on and breathe evenly and regularly while you climb.

CHEATSTONE

If you can't reach the starting holds of a problem you could jump (see page 120), stack a few pads or place a rock (a cheatstone) to help you reach them. The obvious disadvantage of a cheatstone is the risk of falling onto it.

POWERSPOT

A powerspot is when your spotter takes some of your weight so that you can get the feel of a move. It's also a good way to bypass a move you can't do, to allow you to try the moves above it.

ABOVE Tom Peckkitt on Clash of the Titans, Saint Bees, UK. Photo by Dave Gater.

SKIN CARE

Bouldering is very hard on the skin of the hands, especially the fingertips. Not only is it very uncomfortable when your tips get pink and tender, but they don't grip as well, especially on small or slopey holds.

Ideally, the skin on our tips should be smooth - with no points of weakness where tears can start - thick - to make pulling on rough rock and sharp holds more comfortable - and supple - so that it conforms to the tiny indentations in the rock.

Climbing on big holds can give you large callouses which, as well as being uncomfortable, can cause flappers. A flapper is when you rip a large chunk of skin off, usually during a dynamic move. If you are unlucky enough to get one, wash it, press the flap of skin back in place and tape around it so you can continue climbing. Keep callouses in check by regularly filing them down with a pumice stone or fine sandpaper.

Pulling hard on small crimps can create ridges in your skin which can tear and cause the top layer of skin to peel. A quick rub with fine sandpaper will remove the ridge and reduce the chances of it rolling or tearing.

Chalk absorbs the moisture from your hands, so it's vital to keep your skin moisturised. Dry skin is much more likely to split and tear.

There are a few creams/balms that are designed to encourage the growth of new skin and moisturise (Climb On and Palmer's Cocoa Butter are excellent). Get into the habit of washing the chalk off your hands and applying some immediately after climbing.

If you are prone to sweaty hands a product called Antihydral Cream can reduce sweating but it should be used in moderation as it's very powerful.

Looking after your skin is vital on trips. The key is to stop climbing each day before your tips start to get sore, if your skin gets too thin there is little chance it will recover. Avoid sharp or very rough holds, warm-up on the most comfortable holds you can find, make each try count and if faced with a particularly sharp hold consider taping preemptively.

There is no shortcut to good skin, lots of bouldering on rough rock is the only way to build it up.

ABOVE A well used pair of hands. Photo by Florian Oehrlein.

PROJECTS

Some boulderers feel cheated if a problem takes less than a few hundred attempts while others lose interest after a few tries. But if you want to climb a problem at the limit of your ability you have to put the time and effort in.

The process of laying siege to a problem, spending days, weeks or even months learning the moves and getting stronger until you climb it, is known as working a project.

A problem needs to be something special to justify dedicating so much time and energy to it, maybe the lure of the first ascent, an amazing line, great moves or ideally all three.

Consider the following when choosing a project:

- Play to your strengths, projecting isn't the time to work on your weaknesses.

- Avoid problems that are hard on the skin, you will spend more time waiting for your skin to heal than climbing.

- Working problems that are rarely in good condition can be frustrating.

- If you are going to be trying the project on your own then the landing should be pretty good.

- Be realistic about what you are able for. It's better to select an achievable goal, do it and move on to the next problem, than to waste time on something that is out of your league.

- An accessible project will make for a good climbing/travelling ratio.

ABOVE Troy Mattingley on Granular Bastard, West Coast, New Zealand. Photo by Troy Mattingley.

WARMING UP AND DOWN

Warm-up on problems with similar angles, holds and moves to your project. If there aren't any suitable problems to warm-up on nearby, you may have to warm-up elsewhere or use your project to warm-up (do this by hanging the biggest holds and doing the easiest moves - more than once if necessary).

See page 146 for more about warming up.

Spending a large portion of your climbing time on just one problem can have a negative effect on your overall ability as both volume and variety are limited. A circuit of easier problems as a warm down will keep you ticking over.

PREPARE

Time spent planning and preparing before attempting a problem will minimise mistakes and save energy in the long run.

If necessary use a rope, climb a tree or get a shoulder to check and clean the holds. View the problem from as many different angles as possible to make sure you don't miss anything. Pay close attention to the top especially if the problem is high or the top out looks tricky.

WORKING THE MOVES

Gymnastics has a term 'chunking' which means breaking down complicated routines into smaller 'chunks'. Hard boulder problems require a similar approach. Concentrating on each individual move in turn allows you to focus on finding the best/easiest solution.

Even after you have found the best sequence keep an open mind, as you may have overlooked something. It can be helpful to try your project alongside another climber as they may have fresh ideas or spot a better sequence.

It's worth keeping note of your progress and beta, drawing little diagrams or videoing your efforts. Reviewing video can help you to

notice mistakes or refinements.

It's very difficult to know when you are trying a move the best way if you can't do it. Likewise just because you can do a move doesn't mean there isn't an easier way.

Working the moves is a fascinating and sometimes frustrating process, full of red herrings, dead ends, revelations and hard work.

RESTING

Repeatedly trying the same moves is very tiring so it's vital to rest sufficiently between attempts. A good rule of thumb is to rest one minute for each power move. If the problem is long or sustained you may need much longer to recover. More technical, balancy problems can be tried more often without affecting performance.

Don't rest too long or let your muscles get cold, you will lose momentum and risk injury.

Make sure that you are well rested before a day's bouldering. Don't expect to climb well if you are hungover, tired, stressed, hungry or dehydrated.

LINKING

Once you can do each move in isolation it's time to start linking the problem together by practising larger sections.

There is no rule about how long each link should be or how many links you should do, but the goal is to practise just enough so that you climb the full problem on your first try. Make sure the links overlap otherwise you risk missing out moves.

A lot of steep, modern problems start from sitting and often the standing and sitting start are considered distinct problems with their own grades and even names. So at the very least make sure you do the standing start before trying the sitting start.

Linking builds familiarity with moves and how they relate to each other. Sometimes doing

one move in a sub-optimal way will position you so that the next, harder move is possible.

One approach to linking is to try the moves in reverse order ie. do the last move, then start from the second last move etc. until you are ready to attempt the problem from the start.

Make sure that you have the easier sections, especially the top out well rehearsed. Moves that feel easy in isolation can be a different prospect when you are tired.

If it's possible to reach the higher moves, by stepping on from another boulder, a tree or getting a shoulder, take advantage. While the 'ground up' approach helps you get familiar with the initial moves it can mean you are tired by the time you get to the higher moves. And this can make it harder to find the best sequence.

TRAINING

Some boulderers like to beat their project into submission, climbing exclusively on it until it's done.

Others prefer to figure out what they need to improve and then go away and work on those weaknesses, so that when they return they can do the problem relatively quickly. One advantage of this approach is that you don't risk getting frustrated and bored of your project.

FAILURE

Failure is a major part of bouldering especially when you are trying to climb close to your limit.

Staying motivated in the face of constant

ABOVE Kajsa Rosén in Gaisenjarga, Sweden. Photo by Stefan Ösund.

failure can be difficult. Look for even the smallest improvements such as climbing well in bad conditions or sticking a hold for a micro second longer. Once you keep making progress you will get there eventually.

If you mess up the sequence it might be better to step off rather than waste energy and skin battling on. Some problems can be fought up but for others you need to stay in control.

If, after a few unsuccessful attempts, you aren't even getting close, consider whether you need to spend more time practising a section or tweaking the sequence.

After each session think about what you have learnt and make a note of any new beta or refinements of the sequence. Are there any areas (technique or strength) you need to improve?

SENDING

Once you have figured out the moves and have done some good links you are ready to try to climb the problem in its entirety. After putting in the effort, you can be confident that the problem is within your grasp.

The following routine will prepare you so that once you pull onto the problem your focus is 100% on the climbing.

- Check the pads are where you want them and that your spotters are ready.
- Give your shoes a good clean.
- Run through the moves in your head.
- Chalk up.
- Take a few deep breaths and off you go.

ABOVE Nik Goile on Ysgo Slab, Porth Ysgo, UK. Photo by Rob Howell.

9

TRAINING

Climbers' attitudes to training vary hugely. Some religiously follow a training program of Olympic proportions, while the closest others get to training is an occasional visit to the wall where they spend as much time chatting and drinking coffee as climbing.

Whatever your approach to training, it's important to remember that improving is about a lot more than just getting stronger, strength is only one of the many factors that determines your bouldering ability.

It may be a cliché, but the best training for bouldering is bouldering. Beginners in particular should focus on movement, gathering experience by climbing on as many different problems and rock types as possible.

Once your technique is solid, it may be worth spending some training time focussing on strength exercises that target specific areas of weakness (fingers, arms, core). But,

remember that this type of training should be a supplement, rather than a substitute, for actual climbing.

Climbing as an organised competitive sport, is relatively young, and the body of training knowledge and research is tiny compared to other more established sports. The ubiquity of climbing walls means that more people than every are starting to climb. This, combined with rapidly improving training methods explains why standards are increasing, and will continue to increase, at a startling rate.

Training is a huge, complex subject and this chapter only touches on some of the most important aspects of training for bouldering. If you are interested in this area, consult the references on page 191.

PREVIOUS SPREAD The Depot training room, Leeds, UK. Photo by Sebastian Smith.
ABOVE Jamie Emerson campusing in Movement Climbing+ Fitness, Boulder, Colorado, US. Photo by Beau Kahler.

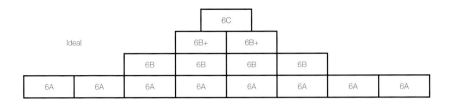

Ideal

				6C			
			6B+	6B+			
		6B	6B	6B	6B		
6A	6A	6A	6A	6A	6A	6A	6A

Too steep

	6C	
6B+	6B+	
6B		
6A	6A	6A

Too low

	6B	6B	6B	6B		
6A	6A	6A	6A	6A	6A	6A

COACHING

Coaching is a relatively new phenomenon in climbing, until recently climbers trained using a mix of trial and error combined with adapted methodologies from other sports.

The rise in popularity of competition climbing, to the point where it's now a discipline in itself, has encouraged a more scientific approach.

Most coaches have experience of climbing and competing at the highest level, but that isn't a guarantee that they will be a good coach. Look for someone who has a deep understanding of climbing movement and is capable of articulating it.

Coaching can also take the form of informal feedback from other climbers. Your fellow climber is in an ideal position to point out things you are doing wrong and suggest ways to correct them.

A lot of walls regularly host workshops, aimed at beginner and intermediate climbers. They are cheaper than one to one coaching and are a good way to learn, as well as to meet other like-minded climbers.

GRADE PYRAMID

A grade pyramid is a very simple, but useful, way of identifying your strengths and weaknesses. They are a list of problems that you have climbed in the last six months or year, ordered by grade.

Ideally the pyramid should form a triangle with a broad base tapering gradually to the hardest ascent at the top (see top).

A tall pyramid with a narrow base or large gaps indicates a lack of climbing experience (see middle). To build a tall pyramid requires a large stable base.

A wide, low pyramid (see bottom) might suggest that you are ready to break into the next level and should spend some time on harder problems.

It's possible to take this idea further and create pyramids for different angles, styles, venues, indoors, outdoors, rock types etc.

Remember that grades are unreliable and are highly subjective, so don't interpret the results too literally. Look at general patterns rather than dwelling on minor anomalies.

WORK YOUR WEAKNESSES

Bouldering performance depends on many factors and often it isn't immediately apparent which factors are limiting progress.

Consider, for example, a climber struggling on a steeply overhanging problem. They are having trouble hanging onto the small holds, let alone moving between them. Their instinct is to blame a lack of finger strength, when it's just as likely to be a weak core or sloppy footwork that is preventing them from transferring their weight onto the foot holds and away from their fingers.

Another example is of a climber that struggles on slabs who, while acknowledging this area of weakness, doesn't realise that the root cause - bad footwork and inability to trust their feet - handicaps every aspect of their climbing.

Weaknesses drag down your overall level and while it's only natural to gravitate towards problems that suit your strengths, to become a better climber you must address your weaknesses.

To establish what those weaknesses are, think about your likes and dislikes, talk to your climbing partners or create a grade pyramid. Don't think exclusively in terms of movement, look at the broader context as well:

- Do you prefer climbing on your own or in a group?
- Are you better at flashing or sieging?
- Do you rely on others for beta?
- Do your tactics let you down?

Once you have identified your weaknesses, the next step is to improve them, this is as simple as devoting some of your climbing time to them.

It requires more effort to make small improvements in areas of strength than it does to make large gains in areas of weakness. This is why working weaknesses is particularly important for climbers who have only limited time to train.

LEFT An Unknown Climber on Black Slabbath, Squamish, Canada. Photo by Thomas Burden.
RIGHT Kristen Ubaldi on Once Upon a Time, Black Mountain, California, US. Photo by Damon Corso.

7A

Current level   6C+   6C+   TARGET LEVEL

6c   6C   6C   6C

6b+   6B+   6B+   6B+   6B+   6B+

6B   6B   6B   6B   6B   6B   6B   6B   6B   6B

GOALS

Goals are vital if you want to improve your climbing, they motivate and give direction to training. The most common goal in bouldering is to climb a specific problem - known as a project (see page 132).

If your goal is to raise your maximum grade then it can be worth looking closely at your grade pyramid. The sample pyramid above illustrates the goal of moving from a maximum grade of 6C to 7A. It shows the importance of broadening the base of the pyramid before attempting to raise it higher.

Monitor your progress towards your goals. And while constantly changing your goals is counter-productive, if your goal isn't right, don't be afraid to change it.

Consider the SMART acronym when setting your goals:

SPECIFIC

It isn't enough just to say "I want to climb harder", be specific, for example "I want to do 6 slabby 6Bs on my trip to Font at Easter".

MEASURABLE

How will you know you have achieved your goal? Goals about "improving foot work" are worthy, but very hard to measure.

ATTAINABLE

A goal should have a reasonable chance of success. Take into account your resources, time and ability.

RELEVANT

A goal that focuses on arm strength, "I want to do a one arm pull up", isn't very relevant if you do most of your climbing on vertical rock.

TIMELY

Set a time limit on your goal. A shorter time frame and a less ambitious goal can be more effective.

TRAINING PLAN

A training plan details and schedules the work that needs to be done to achieve a goal. When drawing up your plan make sure you are realistic about how much time and energy you will be able to dedicate to training. An ambitious plan is useless if it's doomed from the start.

Keep note of your training and climbing sessions so that you can monitor your progress and figure out what's working and what isn't.

EFFORT AND CONSISTENCY

When you start climbing the learning curve is steep and improvement is rapid but after a while it slows down and it requires more and more effort to progress.

If you want to improve it's vital to climb regularly, as training gains, strength in particular, are lost quickly. Start slowly and build up gradually. Jumping into the deep end will only result in injury.

TECHNIQUE TRAINING

If we consider climbing as a language, then our repertoire of moves is equivalent to our vocabulary. And while it's possible to get the point across with a limited vocabulary, in order to express yourself clearly and accurately, a large vocabulary is vital.

However, it's not enough just to know the meaning of each word, you have to use it in the correct context with the right pronunciation etc. This takes practice and the first few times it probably won't come out right.

The same is true for climbing movement, it's impossible to read about a technique and then execute it flawlessly first time, you need to practise and experiment first.

You won't become a better climber just by sitting on the couch reading this (or any other) book, but if you apply what you have read when you are out bouldering, you will be on the right path.

HOW WE LEARN

The initial phase of acquiring a new technique, requires complete concentration. The climber must be free to focus entirely on the mechanics of the new movement. This can only happen on relatively easy moves in a quiet, low pressure environment with a relaxed mind and fresh body.

On hard problems you are likely to perform unfamiliar techniques incorrectly and acquire bad habits or revert to older, more ingrained techniques. This is why it's so important to spend a lot of your time on problems below your limit.

As you gain experience with a new skill, it requires less conscious thought and you will be able to apply it more widely. The skill could be considered mastered when you are able to use it in pressure situations, at your limit. Getting to this point can take months or even years.

LEARNING TECHNIQUE

Technique should be an integral part of each climbing session, not an optional extra.

- Just because you got to the top of a problem doesn't mean you climbed well, there is always something that can be improved. Repeating familiar problems is a great way to fine tune technique.

- Closely observe other climbers. Ask your friends (or even better enemies) for feedback on your technique.

- Plan and analyse every move you make, both successes and failures. Ask yourself what worked, what didn't and why?

- Don't blindly copy other people's sequences, figure it out for yourself.

- Work on your weaknesses. Don't always climb at your limit, make time for sessions when you drop a few grades and tackle a weakness or climb on an angle or style that you have neglected recently.

- Treat grades as only a very rough indicator of which problems you should be able for. Everyone has different strengths and weaknesses and grades can't take this into account.

- Beginners, especially strong ones, gravitate towards steep walls and big holds, a combination that is relatively forgiving of bad body position. Make sure you spend time on less steep angles with small holds where your body position must be good to succeed.

- Boulder outdoors, especially on 'technical' rock ie. slopey, featureless, blank problems that requires cunning and skill rather than raw power.

The following exercises isolate and focus attention on a single aspect of climbing technique.

DOWN CLIMBING

Climbing down problems can offer some interesting insights as well as being good practice for retreating from highballs. Avoid dropping onto hand holds, it can be very stressful for the joints.

SPEED

Climbing very slowly focuses attention on subtle adjustments that might go unnoticed at normal speed.

Moving quickly is a great way of building fluidity and fluency. On longer problems, where stamina is an issue, the ability to move quickly and accurately is very useful.

QUIET FEET

Your feet shouldn't make any noise when you climb. Practise traversing a vertical wall with plenty of foot holds, listening out for the slightest sound. Also get into the habit of placing each foot very accurately and not looking away until it's settled.

NO HANDS

Climbing slabby problems without help from the hands is probably the best way of improving your footwork, balance and body position.

ONE HAND

Traversing with only one hand is one of the best ways to get a feel for the deadpoint - that moment when the body is moving neither up nor down.

ONE FOOT

By limiting yourself to only one foot on the rock at any one time, you force yourself to flag during every move.

OVER-GRIPPING

Over-gripping, squeezing holds harder than necessary, is a bad habit that's caused by fear or anxiety. It wastes energy at a time when it's badly needed.

A good drill is to repeatedly climb a problem, gripping slightly less with the hands each time until eventually you get to a point where you fall off.

CUT LOOSE

The following exercises simultaneously develop both aspects of body tension - core strength and technique (see page 154).

- Find a steep problem with reasonable hand holds. Climb the problem and after each hand move cut loose, kill the swing and then replace your feet.

- Choose a very steep wall with plenty of good hand holds and a pair of small foot holds. Start in a bunched position on the foot holds and move the hands higher up the wall keeping your feet in the same position. The goal is to get your body as stretched out as possible and hold that position for 3-8 seconds.

STATIC / DYNAMIC

If you have either a particularly dynamic or static stye then it can be useful to spend some time climbing in your counter style.

Climbing a steep, juggy problem and hovering your hand over each hold for a few seconds before you grasp it, forces you to climb statically and teaches you about optimal body position as well as giving the arms a good workout.

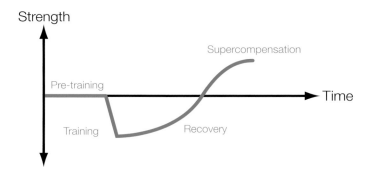

Strength — Time

Supercompensation

Pre-training

Training

Recovery

PHYSICAL TRAINING

Throughout this book the emphasis has been on the importance of movement and technique, nonetheless strength is a critical factor in bouldering ability, especially for experienced climbers who have good technique.

Training stresses and tires the body, but, after a period of recovery, the body responds. The muscles get bigger, tendons strengthen and blood vessels grow to enable the body handle the stresses of training better in the future. This is known as supercompensation.

Timing is key to taking advantage of this phenomenon. If you rest for too long the gains will be lost, and if you don't rest long enough your body won't have fully recovered.

As the body adapts to the demands placed on it, the volume of training must be progressively increased. There are four aspects to volume:

- Quantity, how much climbing you do.
- Intensity, how difficult that climbing is.
- Density, how much rest you take during a workout.
- Frequency, how often you climb.

As climbers improve and climb harder problems, intensity naturally increases, but if performance plateaus then volume needs to be increased in other ways ie. by climbing more frequently, doing more in each session or resting less.

HYPERTROPHY

Hypertrophy means increasing a muscle's size. From a climbing point of view bigger isn't necessarily better, as doubling a muscle's mass only increases its strength by 60%.

Lightly built climbers may benefit from some specific hypertrophy training, but for most climbers time is better spent on other things.

RECRUITMENT

Muscle consists of fibres and each fibre can either be contracted or relaxed. The force produced by a muscle is determined by the number of fibres contracted.

Maximum recruitment is the number of fibres that can be contracted in an all-out effort. Varying levels of maximum recruitment explain why climbers with similar size muscles can differ in strength.

High recruitment is very important to climbers as it has no affect on body weight.

Climbing very powerful problems that are close to your limit is the best way to increase recruitment.

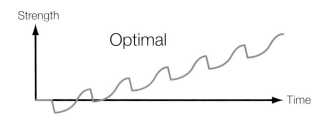

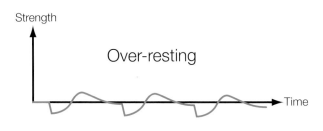

OVER-TRAINING

It's easy to get caught up in a wave of motivation, bouldering and training at every opportunity, but if you don't take sufficient rest between training sessions you risk over-training, and becoming weaker instead of stronger.

The inverse of over-training is over-resting. If the gap between training sessions is too long, the gains made will disappear and you will be back to where you started or even slightly worse. This is why training consistently is so important.

ENDURANCE

Even though most boulder problems take seconds rather than minutes to climb, endurance is still important to boulderers.

Power endurance, the ability to do multiple hard moves in a row, is vital on steep, sustained problems.

On climbing trips the capacity to climb multiple days in a row and recover quickly is vital if you want to make the best use of limited time.

Maintaining a high performance level through a long training session allows a larger volume of training to be done, which improves endurance allowing more training.

WARMING-UP

A thorough warm-up is essential if you want to climb well and avoid injury. It increases blood flow and lubricates the joints as well as focusing the mind on the task in hand.

Develop a good warm-up routine and follow it diligently. Be patient as it can take up to an hour before you are ready to climb at your limit.

Use your warm-up to gauge how well you are climbing and adapt your plans accordingly.

STAY WARM

Once you are well warmed up make sure you don't cool down while you rest. Throw on a warm jacket and hat and walk around to keep the blood flowing. If you do cool down, do a short warm-up before jumping back onto a hard problem.

WARM-UP TOOLS

A length of stretchy elastic (theraband) can be helpful for warming up, especially if there aren't any suitable easy problems. Some climbers squeeze a rubber ball to get the blood flowing to their fingers and hands.

WARMING DOWN

After a hard session your muscles will be full of lactic acid and toxins that hinder recovery and cause stiffness. Ten minutes of easy bouldering or traversing will encourage blood flow and flush them out.

A banana and some water will replace lost fluids and energy, also helping promote recovery.

The best time to work on your flexibility is immediately after you have finished climbing, while you are still warm. See page 158 for more about stretching.

HOW TO WARM-UP

There are four stages to a good warm-up:

1 PULSE RAISER

The walk to the boulders, a short jog or skipping will get the blood flowing. A few minutes is sufficient.

2 STRETCHING

Gently move your fingers, wrists, elbows, shoulders, neck, back, legs, hips, and ankles through their ranges of motion, focussing on the upper body.

Remember that your goal is to lubricate the joints and loosen the muscles, you aren't trying to increase your range of motion (do that when you are finished climbing).

Avoid using static stretching (see page 158) as part of your warm-up as it reduces the amount of power the muscles can produce.

3 CLIMBING

Start by climbing some very easy problems or traversing on big holds, focusing on moving well. Gradually increase the difficulty, taking plenty of rest between problems.

If there are no easy problems to warm-up on, look for big holds to hang from or just find the easiest moves you can and repeat them. Alternatively warm-up at another area or the climbing wall.

The problems that you warm-up on should be similar (moves, holds, angle, length etc) to those you are planning to attempt later in the session.

INJURIES

Injuries are one of the most frustrating aspects of bouldering, and while serious injuries are rare, elbow and finger problems are all too common. However, if you develop good habits and a patient, sensible approach your chances of injury will be dramatically reduced.

This chapter gives only a brief overview, see page 191 for a list of books that cover climbing injuries in more detail.

The information in this section shouldn't be used a substitute for attending a medical professional for correct assessment, advice and rehabilitation of injuries. If you have any doubts about an injury talk to a professional, ideally one that knows something about climbing.

Bouldering injuries can be divided into two categories - acute and chronic.

ACUTE

In bouldering an acute injury is one that is caused by an accident, usually a fall. Acute injuries aren't that common, but they can be severe. If you are in any doubt about the seriousness of an injury, don't hesitate to seek medical help immediately.

If you climb in remote areas a first aid course is worth considering.

CHRONIC

Chronic injuries are caused by overuse or misuse and are much more common than acute injuries. Tendons and ligaments take years to adapt to the stress and strains of intensive bouldering, so it's vital for beginners to start out slowly and focus on technique rather than strength for the first few years.

PREVENTION

The old cliché 'prevention is better than cure' is very relevant, especially as climbing injuries have a habit of never really going away.

So what can be done to reduce the chances of getting injured?

- Warm-up well, see page 146 for more information.
- Strengthen the antagonistic muscles, see the next page for details.
- Constantly climbing on the same angle and holds, places a lot of stress on a very small number of muscles and tendons. A varied diet of climbing will help spread the load.
- Increase volume and intensity gradually otherwise you risk overtraining (page 145) and soft tissue injuries.
- Stay hydrated. Tendons are much more likely to get damaged when they are dry.
- Listen carefully to your body. Be particularly alert at the end of a session when you are tired and your movement has started to get sloppy. Don't be afraid to change your plans. If your fingers are sore after your warm-up, is it wise to spend the session working your crimpy project?
- Certain activities, moves and holds are more likely to cause injury for example campus boarding, some fingerboarding, weighted pull ups, big dynos, gastons, finger pockets etc. All should be approached with extreme caution.

THE ANTAGONISTIC MUSCLES

Muscles work in pairs, as one muscles contracts, the other relaxes. Climbing generally demands more from the pulling than the pushing (antagonistic or opposition) muscles.

As your climbing muscles strengthen an imbalance develops that places a lot of strain on the joints, tendons and ligaments. This can be the cause of injuries especially to the elbows and shoulders.

A workout comprising of pushing exercises such as press ups, dips, external shoulder rotations, low rows and reverse wrist curls done a few times a week will address any muscle imbalance. Stretching is also important, as muscles shorten as they strengthen, see page 158.

REHAB AND RECOVERY

When recovering from an injury patience is key. It's natural to want to get back to climbing as quickly as possible, but if you start back too soon before the injury has had sufficient time to fully recover, you risk re-injury and further delaying your return to climbing.

Wait until all swelling, tenderness and pain are gone, before you start back with some easy climbing on large holds. Progressively increase the difficulty, easing off if there is any pain, until you are back up to full speed.

TAPE

Some climbers use finger (zinc oxide) tape to give some extra support to recovering or troublesome tendons. It's unclear whether this is effective. Some say it gives support, while others claim that it prevents the taped area from strengthening.

From the physiological point of view there is a danger that taping can give a false sense of security, but on the other hand, it can serve as a visual reminder to go easy on the injured area.

FINGERS

Climbing is unique among sports/activities in that it places huge stress on the fingers and, unfortunately, finger injures, specifically tendon damage are very common in bouldering.

Most finger injuries occur in the pulleys, a band of fibres that hold the tendons in the fingers close to the bone, particularly the A2 pulley which lies between the base of the finger and the middle knuckle.

Most finger injuries are sustained in one of the following ways:

- The accumulation of micro-trauma over time due to misuse/overuse, which gradually becomes increasingly painful.
- Unexpectedly overloading the fingers, often because of a foot slip or a badly coordinated slap. The joint may make an audible pop, and there may be immediate pain and swelling.

The tendons in the fingers take years to adapt to the rigours of bouldering, so if you rush into an intensive training regime you greatly increase the chances of finger problems.

Beginners, in particular should avoid crimping, campus boarding and repeatedly attempting dynamic moves on small holds as they are very hard on the fingers.

As the fingers generally receive poor blood flow finger injuries can take a long time to heal. A long break, finger strengthening and a gradual return to climbing is the only answer.

WRISTS

Wrist injuries aren't that common but open handed holds, pockets and undercuts can cause problems.

Spending too much time in front of the computer can cause repetitive strain issues in the wrists.

ELBOWS

Pains in the inside (golfer's elbow) and outside (tennis elbow) of the elbows are common, they are caused by a lack of balance between pushing and pulling muscles. Certain moves such as gastons, deep lock offs and exercises such as campus boarding and weighted pull ups can put a huge amount of strain on the elbows and cause problems.

Over-training and bad technique can also be the cause of some elbow problems.

Pushing down hard on sloping holds with a slightly bent arm causes 'Font elbow', named after the Fontainebleau bouldering area which is notorious for its sloping holds.

The vast majority of elbow injuries are either tendonitis or tendonosis. Tendonitis is an inflammatory condition arising from acute aggravation. Tendonosis is a degeneration of the tendon itself, arising from micro-trauma inflicted by a muscle that is too strong.

Diagnosis is complicated, but as a rule of thumb, if the pain is sharp it's tendonitis and if it's a dull ache it's tendonosis.

Fortunately there are some basic strengthening exercises that can be done to strengthen the antagonistic muscles which should clear up most elbow aches and pains (see references on page 191).

SHOULDERS

Shoulder injuries are caused by muscle imbalances in the chest and upper back (specifically in the pectoral, rhomboids, middle and lower trapezius, and external rotators). Certain moves (long dynamics, cross throughs and gastons) can place a lot of leverage and strain on the weak, imbalanced shoulder joint and this can cause tendinitis, dislocation or even rotator cuff injuries.

Prevent these problems by stretching the pectorals and strengthening the shoulder girdle and the external rotators.

If your shoulders aren't working well then the muscles in the lower arm have to work harder, potentially causing problems in the elbow and wrist.

RICE

In the event of a soft tissue injury (sprain, strain, muscle pull, or tear) that causes swelling, follow the RICE mnemonic to reduce swelling, relieve pain and improve the recovery time:

REST

Immediately stop climbing.

ICE

Cold provides pain relief and limits swelling by reducing blood flow to the injured area. A bag of frozen peas wrapped in a towel is ideal, but don't apply it for more than 10 minutes at a time.

COMPRESSION

A snug, but not so tight that you cut off the circulation, bandage will limit swelling.

ELEVATION

Raise the injured area to drain excess fluid and control swelling.

TRAINING INDOORS

Some climbers see indoor climbing as an end in itself while for others it's a necessary evil and not 'real' climbing. However, most boulderers would agree that indoor bouldering is an essential training tool.

TRAINING POWER

The best ways of developing power is by attempting hard problems, especially if they are steep, with small holds and basic (as opposed to technical) moves.

Most climbers approach indoor bouldering in much the same way as they do outdoors - starting with a good warm-up before working a few hard problems, with plenty of rest between attempts.

TRAINING POWER ENDURANCE

One method of building power endurance on a bouldering wall is called 'on the minute'. Find six powerful problems and give yourself one minute to climb and rest after each one. Doing each problem once is a set. Take five minutes rest after each set and repeat.

It can take some experimentation to gauge the difficulty of the problems. If you get it right you should be just able to complete the last problem in each set.

OTHER TRAINING TOOLS

The following training tools can be found at most climbing walls and even in some climber's homes.

TRAINING BOARD

Training boards are small, steep bouldering walls, that are covered in an array of mostly wooden holds (see facing page). Originally built in cellars, attics and spare rooms, nowadays most climbing centres also have one.

As they are steep (around 45°) and the holds are small, they aren't suitable for beginners.

Each hold is given a unique number, so that climbers can set and record problems, that simulate projects and train specific weaknesses.

If you have some space in your house it's relatively straightforward to build a board. The convenience of not having to leave the house to train makes even a small board a powerful training tool.

SYSTEM BOARD

A system board is a steep board on which the various hold types - pinch, edge, sloper, pocket, undercut, sidepull - are laid out in a repeating, symmetrical pattern. This allows very specific movements, hold types and orientations to be targeted and trained.

System boards make good use of limited space and the basic principle can easily be applied on a small training board.

CAMPUS BOARD

A campus board is a small wall covered at regular intervals with wooden rungs (see page 138). There are a range of footless exercises that can be done on them, ranging from laddering up the rungs to dramatic double dynos.

Campusing is very high intensity and isn't suitable for beginners, in fact the British Mountaineering Council advises under 18s against using them and warns everyone that "campus boarding can seriously damage your fingers!".

FACING PAGE Ben Read at the Arch Climbing Wall, London, UK Photo by Aneta Parchanska.

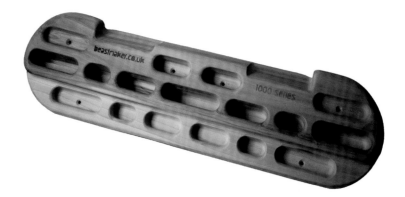

FINGERBOARDING

Strong fingers are important and the most effective method of strengthening them is hanging from small holds (deadhanging).

It takes years of climbing before the tendons and ligaments in the fingers are ready for the rigours of fingerboarding, so it isn't suitable for beginners, who are better off working on their movement skills.

Fingerboarding requires a good warm-up and a patient, progressive approach if injury is to be avoided.

FINGERBOARDS

Although it's possible to do a fingerboard session using holds on a steep wall or rungs on a campus board, a purpose built fingerboard (see above) is the best tool for the job.

Making a simple fingerboard is reasonably straightforward, all you need are a few wooden edges and some plywood. Make sure the edges are rounded and splinter free.

Mounting a fingerboard over a doorway at home allows you to get a useful workout in as little as a half hour.

PROGRESSION

As your fingers get stronger you need to increase the load to keep making strength gains. Very small holds are more likely to

cause injuries so once you are comfortable on a flat 20mm edge with two hands, it's time to add weight or do one-handed hangs on a larger hold.

To hang one handed you will, initially, need help on anything but jugs. Reduce the load using a simple pulley system (see right of the facing page).

For two handed hangs increase the load by hanging weights from a harness (see left of the facing page), or wearing a weight belt or vest.

The advantage of these methods is that they are easily quantifiable and adjustable.

INJURY PREVENTION

- Warm-up well.
- Focus on open hand and half crimp grips and avoid full crimping.
- Load the fingers smoothly and gradually. Avoid pull ups or campus moves on a fingerboard.
- Keep good form while hanging, making sure there is a slight bend in your elbows and that your shoulders aren't slumped together.
- Fingerboarding is very intensive so don't over do it, less is more.

HOW TO

Warm-up (pulse raiser, range of motion exercises, stretch the fingers, arms, shoulders) before starting off with some gentle two-handed hangs on the largest holds, taking weight off if necessary.

As you feel yourself getting stronger gradually move onto the smaller holds, adding weight or hanging one handed.

Choose holds that you can hang for between five and eight seconds, this is the optimal hang time for strength gains, if you can hang

significantly longer then the hold is too big.

Rest for at least a minute between each hang. A few hangs on each hand is sufficient, stop or move onto a different grip or hold type before you start to tire.

Remember you are training strength not endurance. A few sessions a week is plenty, especially if you are also bouldering.

PREPARING FOR ROCK

Indoor walls will never exactly replicate the subtleties of bouldering on rock, so if your priority is to climb well outdoors, focus your indoor training on problems that:

- Feature very small foot holds.
- Involve pushing and pressing rather than just pulling straight down.
- Have plenty of possible sequences and holds to consider.

If your local wall lacks suitable problems, either request that some are set or make up your own. This is when a good training board (see page 151) comes into its own. The density and variety of holds allows you to create problems tailored to your requirements.

CIRCUITS

A circuit is a grouping of (usually around 20) problems of similar difficulty, but diverse styles. Most good indoor walls will have a range of circuits set by experienced climbers.

Completing an easy circuit is an excellent way to warm-up or to get some mileage in at the end of a session. As most circuits are left on the wall for months they are also a good way of benchmarking progress.

TRAINING OUTDOORS

If you are fortunate enough to have access to good outdoor bouldering year round, there probably isn't much need to climb indoors. Your strength and, more importantly, your technique will improve without any training other than 'just' climbing.

The potential downside is that - due to skin issues, weather or the style of climbing - it can be difficult to get a good physical workout. Seeking out powerful problems or making an occasional visit to the wall should help restore the balance.

As with climbing indoors variety is important. Travel around, visit other areas, climb on a variety of rock types and angles.

TRAINING OR PERFORMING?

It's vital, especially if you climb outdoors a lot, to understand the difference between training and performing. Scottish climber Dave MacLeod compares training to saving money and performing to spending it, naturally spending must be preceded by a period of saving.

TRAINING

Training includes things like working a project, addressing a weakness, doing a long circuit of easy problems, re-climbing problems you have done before or trying to complete a few hard problems in a day.

PERFORMING

You are performing when you are attempting to push your limits, for example when you are working the moves or trying to link a hard project.

WEIGHT

Strength to weight ratio is hugely important in climbing, and as a result some climbers become obsessed with their weight, falling into the trap of believing that losing a few pounds will make all the difference.

Once you are a healthy weight, using weight loss to improve performance is an unsustainable measure, and is a dangerous and unhealthy road to go down. However if you are overweight, losing some weight should have a positive influence on your climbing and your general health.

CORE

A climber's core (primarily the abdominal and lower back muscles) is the link between their hand and foot holds, so a strong core is incredibly important for climbers, particularly on steep rock.

Body tension is the ability to transmit power between the feet and hands, strong fingers and arms aren't much use without it. Core strength is one component of body tension, the other is technique.

Exercises such as front levers, leg raises (see page 157), supermans and planks (see page 156) will strengthen the core, while steep bouldering on small foot holds and the drills on page 143 target body tension.

CROSS TRAINING

Cross training is doing another sport or activity as training for bouldering.

Bouldering uses very specific muscles and movements, so spending time doing other sports and activities will have health benefits that extend outside climbing. However, cross training can also have some climbing-specific benefits.

If you train hard for most of the year then taking a break from bouldering for a few weeks can be helpful for both the mind and body. And hopefully you will return well-rested and full of motivation.

Activities that use the upper body like swimming, kayaking or surfing, will strengthen the core and the antagonistic muscles (see page 148).

Light aerobic activity such as hiking, running or cycling increases blood circulation and speeds up recovery between climbing sessions.

ABOVE Audrey Seguy at the Castle Climbing Centre, London, UK. Photo by Aneta Parchanska.

Regular aerobic exercise, along with eating less, is also the most effective way to lose excess weight.

Climbing is quite a specialised activity, and while there are benefits to cross training, unless you have a lot of time to dedicate to training, you should focus on more climbing-specific activities.

YOGA

Both yoga and bouldering make similar demands on balance, strength, technique, flexibility, body awareness and inner calm. Some walls run yoga classes specifically aimed at climbers, which are an enjoyable way to improve your flexibility, posture etc.

FLOOR EXERCISES

The following exercises are excellent for overall strength. And even though they aren't climbing specific, they have an important role to play in injury prevention by strengthening the antagonistic muscles (see page 148).

Some of these exercises can place a lot of strain on your back so if it's sore or you have back problems consult a professional first.

SIT UPS

Sit ups target the upper abdominal muscles which aren't that important for climbing. They won't do any harm but there are more useful exercises for climbers.

PUSH UPS

Push ups (aka press ups) are a great general exercise that work the pushing muscles, which can be neglected, particularly if you do a lot of indoor climbing.

Remember to keep the body straight and rigid throughout the movement. By varying the position of your hands you can target different muscles.

Push ups are particularly effective at alleviating elbow problems and pain.

PISTOLS

A pistol is a one leg squat. They are great for building the power, balance and coordination required for difficult rockovers.

Start standing on one leg and slowly sink down until your bottom is nearly touching the ground. Keep your other leg straight out in front and make sure that your foot stays flat on the ground. Now press up back to a standing position, if this is too difficult, push off a wall or use a door frame for assistance.

The following isometric (static) exercises involve assuming and holding a position for as long as possible.

PLANK

The plank is an excellent exercise for the core, shoulders and arms. There are many variations, but the standard front plank involves getting in a push up position, but instead of resting on your hands, you rest on your forearms. Hold your back completely straight while trying to hold your abs in.

For a side plank, lie on your right side, propped up on your elbow. Rest your left foot on top of your right, and push up so that your body forms a triangle with the floor. Hold as long as possible and repeat on the other side.

SUPERMANS

Start on your hands and feet and simultaneously lift one arm, pointing it straight ahead while extending the opposite leg straight backwards. Return to the starting position and mirror the movement with the opposite arm and leg.

SPIDERMANS

The Spiderman is a great body tension exercise. Start in a push up position and move your legs and arms outwards until your body is as close as possible to the floor. The further out your hands and feet, the harder it is to hold the position.

BAR EXERCISES

It's possible to get a good, but not very climbing specific, upper body workout using just a pull up bar. And while a good base of strength is useful, don't fixate on stunts like one arm pull ups, there are many world class climbers who can't do them.

Use the frontal grip (palms facing away from the body) for these exercises, it's more climbing-specific.

PULL UPS

Pull ups are good for general pulling power, but watch out as overdoing them can cause elbow problems. As you pull up draw the shoulder blades towards the spine and never drop down onto straight arms.

Varying the distance between your hands works different muscles, shoulder width is standard. Pull ups done with the legs or knees bent at 90° gives the core muscles more of a workout.

LOCK OFFS

A lock off is holding a hanging position with the elbows bent at full lock, 45°, 90° or 135°. Strong climbers will be able to do them with one arm. Lock offs can be combined with pull ups to create a slightly more climbing specific exercise.

FRONT LEVER

A front lever is a static hold in which the body is held in a horizontal position with the arms straight. They are one of the best all-round exercises working the core, lower back, triceps and legs.

Levers are difficult, but there are easier versions that can be used as stepping stones. The tuck front lever is when both legs are brought up to the chest and the single leg front lever is done with one leg bent and the other straight (*see above*).

LEG RAISES

A good exercise for the legs and lower core. Hang from the bar and slowly raise your knees to your chest. A harder variation is to raise the feet to waist height while keeping the legs straight.

DIPS

Dips work the triceps, shoulders, chest and back and are great training for mantels, stemming and press moves. They can be done between two chairs, on parallel bars or with a pair of gymnastic rings.

ABOVE Ian Dunne front levering at Awesome Walls, Dublin, Ireland.

FLEXIBILITY

Good flexibility opens more body positioning possibilities and allows you to climb more efficiently. For most climbers flexibility isn't a limiting factor, but if you struggle on high steps and wide bridging moves then some stretching could be useful.

Upper body flexibility is rarely an issue but it's still important to stretch, because as muscles strengthen they become shorter, especially muscles that are recovering from injury.

Like any exercise, if you feel any pain or discomfort during these stretches, stop immediately and consider getting a physiotherapist to recommend an alternative.

TYPES OF FLEXIBILITY

Passive flexibility describes the maximum range of motion of a joint, while active flexibility is the range of motion you are able to access using muscle strength alone.

Normally stretching uses gravity or other aids to stretch, but when climbing our limbs are moved into position by our muscles, thus active flexibility is much more relevant to climbing.

Improving climbing-specific flexibility has two parts, increasing the range of motion (passive stretching) and strengthening the muscles so that they can access the new range of motion (active stretching).

WARMING UP

A proper warm-up before stretching is vital, as cold muscles don't stretch well and you risk injury. A few minutes of gentle exercise to get the blood flowing, followed by some gentle rotation of the limbs through their range of motion is sufficient.

STRETCHING

Flexibility is improved by lengthening the muscles. The stretch reflex prevents muscles from expanding when they are stretched

suddenly. Stretching overcomes this reflex using gentle progressive stretches. Stretching shouldn't be painful but it may be mildly uncomfortable.

To get the most benefit from stretching it's important to do it regularly, ideally every day. The best time to stretch for flexibility is after a climbing session when your muscles are already well warmed up.

PASSIVE STRETCHING

The simplest stretching technique is to slowly and steadily lengthen the muscle. Assume the relevant position and gradually lengthen the muscles over 15 seconds until you are close to your limit, and then hold this position for another 15 seconds. Rest for a minute and repeat twice. Remember to breathe easily and don't bounce or jerk.

There are hundreds of different stretches, consult a stretching text for some specific stretches focusing on the hamstring, hip turnout, groin, pectoral and forearm muscles.

See the facing page for a few suggestions.

ACTIVE STRETCHING

Active stretches develop the strength required to access the limits of passive flexibility.

The way to go about these stretches is by lifting your limb to its limit and then letting go, trying to hold the limb in position for about 10 seconds.

There is scope for more climbing specific active stretches. For example - stand with one foot on the ground with your toe touching the wall. Place your hands on the highest hold that you can reach and try to place your foot onto every foot hold in range.

FACING PAGE
Ian Dunne at Awesome Walls, Dublin, Ireland.

10
DESTINATIONS

GRITSTONE

Sandwiched between the cities of Manchester and Sheffield lies the Peak District, an area that is home to thousands of boulder problems on the famous gritstone. Further north in Yorkshire, there is even more bouldering, rivalling the Peak in terms of both quality and quantity.

Gritstone is a sandy, rough grained sandstone known to the locals as God's own rock. Holds, which are few and far between, are frequently very rounded and exploiting the excellent friction is often the key to success.

There is a long history of bold traditional routes on grit, many of which could be considered highball boulder problems when attempted with multiple pads.

Like sandstone, conditions have a huge bearing on how difficult problems on grit feel. The best friction is to be found in the winter, but spring and autumn offer slightly more reliable weather and longer days.

The grit is only a few hours north of London on the motorway or by train. A few areas are accessible by public transport but a car would open up your options.

Yorkshire Gritstone Bouldering Volume 1, published by Total Climbing covers the major areas in Yorkshire (Volume 2 covers the more obscure areas) and the Peak is beautifully documented in *Peak District Bouldering* by Vertebrate Publishing.

There is, of course, lots of other great bouldering in the UK in North Wales, The Lake District, Northumberland and Scotland.

All of the above areas and many more are described in *Boulder Britain* by Niall Grimes.

PREVIOUS SPREAD Dan Varian on Cypher, Slipstones, Yorkshire, UK. Photo by Nick Brown.
ABOVE Andy Banks on Adults Only, Stanage, UK. Photo by John Coefield.
FACING PAGE Michal Madera on Not to be Taken Away, Stanage, UK. Photo by Michal Madera.

FONTAINEBLEAU

Fontainebleau, just south of Paris, is probably the best bouldering area in the world. More than any other area, it has something for everyone, from easy circuits suitable for children to some of the hardest problems in the world.

While the impeccable sandstone offers the full range of angles and climbing styles, Font is best known for its slopers which require excellent technique, body positioning and footwork.

The rock is very fine grained, so is relatively kind to the skin.

Conditions are best in winter and it gets hot in summer, but it's possible to climb all year round. Spring and autumn are the most popular times to visit.

The generally good (often sandy) landings, abundance of easy problems and the short, flat walk-ins make Font a very family friendly climbing destination.

Circuits, a grouping of problems of similar difficulty, with the problems and descents marked by small arrows painted on the rock, are a speciality of Font. To complete even an easy circuit in a session is a serious workout and will require a wide range of techniques.

The town of Fontainebleau is only a short train journey from the centre of Paris and even though it's possible to walk to a few areas from the train station your choice is limited without a car.

There are dozens of guidebooks to Font, John Watson's pocket sized *Essential Fontainebleau* will tell you everything you need to know.

ABOVE Peter Kußler on Éclipse, Cul de Chien, Fontainebleau, France. Photo by Rolf Seitz.
FACING PAGE Kevin Lopata on Haute Tension, Fontainebleau, France. Photo by Pierre-Alexandre Pheulpin.

ALBARRACÍN

Albarracín in central Spain is one of the best areas in Europe. Scattered about the pine forests just outside the town are red sandstone boulders and cliff edges.

The bouldering is physical in style with a lot of roof climbing and sloping holds. The majority of the problems are in the 5 to 7b range.

If you fly into Madrid or Valencia the drive to Albarracín takes between three or four hours.

Albarracín is at an altitude of 1200m so it's cool enough to climb for most of the year except mid-summer. The climate is very dry so there isn't much rain or snow.

Some of the bouldering sectors have access restrictions between January and August, so autumn is probably the best time to visit. The town of Albarracín has a long and interesting history and the narrow, winding streets are well worth exploring on a rest day.

The most comprehensive guide is *Boulder Albarracín* published by Desnivel which contains details of over 1600 problems.

ABOVE Tom Russell, unknown problem, Albarracín, Spain. Photo by Alex Gorham.
FACING PAGE Roberto Iglesias on Corona, Albarracín, Spain. Photo by Jorge Crespo.

TICINO

The Italian speaking canton of Ticino in the south of Switzerland has over a dozen bouldering areas in close proximity. The rock is predominantly granite (with some gneiss) ranging from very rounded, river smoothed rock to rough mountain stone.

Cresciano has about 900 problems on excellent grey granite boulders set among sweet chestnut trees.

Chironico is at a slightly higher altitude to Cresciano and the boulders are also set among woodland. The rock is gneiss which is more featured and has more small crimps

than granite. The climbing tends to be a little less technical and more physical.

Magic Wood (AKA Averstal) is in the German speaking canton of Graubünden. The gneiss boulders are scattered across a wooded hillside and above a stream that runs down the valley.

San Gottardo Pass and the nearby Sustenpass offer excellent problems on rough granite. The landings are generally good and the rock is high friction crystalline granite set amid very scenic grassy alpine meadows.

The low lying valleys of Chironico and Cresciano are best in spring and autumn

while the high alpine meadows of San Gottardo Pass and Sustenpass are only free of snow in the summer. Magic Wood is unusual in that it gets reasonably good conditions in the summer thanks to the permafrost that lies beneath the boulders.

One of the best things about this region is that it's possible to move from area to area to find the best conditions.

The closest major airport is Milan (Zurich is another option), from there it's a few hours drive over the border. A car would be indispensable if you want to visit more than one area.

Crescianoboulder, *Chironicoboulder*, *Gottardoboulder* cover the respective areas. *Swiss Bloc 1* published by Gebro Verlag documents the northern part of the region including Magic Wood, San Gottardo Pass and Sustenpass.

ABOVE Théo Chappex climbing in Ticino, Switzerland. Photo by David Rigaud.
FACING PAGE Steven Alexander on the Ecstasy Boulder, San Gottardo, Switzerland. Photo by Alex Gorham.

BISHOP

The town of Bishop on the eastern slopes of the Sierra Nevada mountains in California is surrounded by some of the most scenic bouldering in the world.

The bouldering can be divided into two categories. The Happy and Sad boulders consist of volcanic tuff, a featured rock with lots of incut holds and pockets. While the massive granite-like monzonite eggs of The Buttermilks require a more technical style on slopers and small crimps.

The jewel in the crown of Bishop bouldering is the Peabody Boulders. The huge, rounded eggs contain over 600 problems. Many, but not all, are extremely highball on generally positive holds.

An hour's drive to the north is the ski resort of Mammoth Lakes and there is lots of sport and alpine climbing close to Bishop. And the climbing mecca of Yosemite is only a few hours drive north.

Fly into either Reno, LA or San Francisco and drive to Bishop. It's possible to get to Bishop on the bus, but without a car it would be very difficult to travel between the various areas.

From October to May the conditions are usually excellent. The area surrounding the small town of Bishop is in the rain shadow of the Sierra Nevada mountains. Temperatures are mild during the day but once the sun sets it cools down very quickly.

Bishop Bouldering by Wills Young is the definitive guidebook to the area and contains over two thousand problems.

ABOVE An unknown climber on Evilition, Bishop. Photo by Tony Symanovich.
FACING PAGE Nalle Hukkataival on Saigon, Bishop. Photo by Reinhard Fichtinger.

HUECO TANKS

The 860 acre Hueco Tanks State Historical Park near El Paso, Texas is home to some of America's finest bouldering.

The climbing is on featured syenite boulders and outcrops, it's very physical in style and most problems are steep and powerful on small crimps and pockets.

The park contains many important rock paintings some of which are thousands of years old. In the mid nineties the park authorities restricted access to protect the paintings.

Nowadays, access for climbers is still limited, however it's possible to enjoy the great bouldering, you just need to be well organised and patient. During busy holiday periods it's essential to make reservations as there is only a limited number of slots available.

The best time to visit is from October through March. As Hueco is in the desert the weather is usually dry and mild during the day, but cold at night.

The best guide is *Guidebook Hueco Tanks: The Essential Guide* by Matt Wilder.

ABOVE Nina Williams on Babyface, Hueco, Texas, US. Photo by Beau Kahler.
FACING PAGE Patrick Smithson on See Spot Run, Hueco, Texas, US. Photo by Seamus Allan.

SQUAMISH

Less than an hour from Vancouver, Canada lies the town of Squamish. A massive granite monolith, the Stawamus Chief, looms over the town. In the forests at the foot of the Chief lie over 2500 problems on granite boulders.

The rock is rough, blank granite and the climbing style is technical with lots of heel hooking, pinching, palming and smearing.

Thanks to the west coast climate and the shade created by the massive, old growth forest, Squamish is one the best summer bouldering areas in North America.

Squamish is only a short journey from Vancouver, and it's possible to visit without a car, as a lot of the bouldering is within walking distance of the town and the campsite.

The best guidebook is *Squamish Bouldering* by Marc Bourdon, which also covers the bouldering in nearby Whistler and Pemberton.

LEFT Pamela Bourdon on Detached Flake, Squamish, Canada. Photo by Marc Bourdon.
RIGHT Pamela Bourdon on Hydrogen, Squamish, Canada. Photo by Marc Bourdon.
FACING PAGE Sarah Clark on Lounge Act, Squamish, Canada. Photo by Thomas Burden.

CASTLE HILL

Castle Hill, on the South Island of New Zealand, has a huge number of amazing limestone boulders.

The rock is relatively low friction and smooth so the bouldering is both technical and powerful, and can take some getting used to. Castle Hill is notorious for its hard, blank, mantel-shelf top outs.

The area known as Castle Hill is actually composed of many different bouldering areas including: Quantum Field (the most popular area), Dry Valley, Flock Hill (the largest area, but it's a longer walk) and Spittle Hill.

The most popular time to visit is between December and February, but the best conditions are to be found between June and August. Castle Hill lies in a sheltered basin in the rain shadow of the nearby mountains, so conditions are kind - it's the last place to get rain and there's never much wind.

Castle Hill is 1.5 hours drive north west of Christchurch.

Comprehensive Castle Hill Climbing Guide by Matt Pierson and Alan Davison contains details of over 5000 problems.

ABOVE Giani Clement on Orifice Fish 3, Quantum Field, Castle Hill, New Zealand. Photo by Devlin Gandy.
FACING PAGE James Morris on Acapulco, Flock Hill, Castle Hill, New Zealand. Photo by Devlin Gandy.

ROCKLANDS

The Rocklands in South Africa are a few hours drive north of Cape Town in the Cederberg Mountains. The orange and black streaked sandstone boulders have generally good landings and solid holds which makes them ideal for highballs and steep, powerful test pieces. The climbing style in Rocklands is quite gymnastic, featuring lots of big moves between fairly good holds.

While there is a lack of established easy problems there is huge potential for new problems at every grade.

Due to its remote location Rocklands probably isn't suitable for a short visit, but once you are there it's cheap, making it an ideal destination for an a long trip.

A car is essential as Rocklands is very remote and the bouldering areas are spread over a large area.

The most popular time to visit is during June, July and August. The climate is dry and warm, but there can be long spells of rain.

The guidebook, *Rocklands Bouldering*, by Scott Noy describes over a 1000 problems.

ABOVE Nina Williams on Vanity, Rocklands. Photo by Richard Tyler Gross.
FACING PAGE David Mason on Kingdom in the Sky, Rocklands. Photo by Nick Brown.

GLOSSARY

A

Antagonistic The antagonistic muscles are those responsible for pushing as opposed to pulling.

Antihydral A skin drying agent that reduces the hand's sweating.

Ape Index The difference between your arm span and height.

Approach Shoe A hybrid between a running shoe and a hiking boot.

Arch The arched middle part of the sole of the foot that lies between the toes and the ankle. Or a steeply overhanging arete.

Arete A protruding rock feature that is formed by the meeting of two planes. The opposite to a corner.

Arm Bar A crack climbing technique in which an arm is inserted deep into the crack and secured by pressing the palm of the hand against one wall and the tricep/shoulder against the other.

B

Backstep A technique in which one foot inside edges while the other outside edges. Similar to a dropknee.

Back and Foot A method of climbing chimneys in which the back is pressed against one side while the feet push against the other.

Barndoor An unintentional, uncontrolled rotation away from the rock.

Belaying Paying out or taking in the rope while another climber climbs.

Beta A description of how to climb a specific problem, usually refers to the best (ie. easiest) way.

Body Tension The ability to keep the feet on their foot holds when climbing steep rock. Core strength and technique are components of body tension.

Body Position The position of the body relative to the hand and foot holds.

Bolt On A resin or wood hold that is bolted to the surface of a climbing wall.

Boss A rounded lump protruding from the rock that can be used as a hand hold.

Bouldering Pad A rectangular crash mat that consists of multiple layers of foam covered in a heavy duty material. The pad is placed where the climber is expected to fall to cushion their landing (AKA bouldering mat).

Bicycle A technique in which one foot pushes a hold conventionally while the other foot toe hooks the same, or a nearby, hold. Most commonly used when climbing roofs (AKA clamp).

Break A horizontal, often rounded, crack.

Bridging Pushing onwards with the hands and/or feet. Usually done in corners or grooves, but can also be done between two protruding holds (AKA stemming).

Buildering Bouldering on buildings or other man-made structures.

Bulge A rounded roof or overhang.

Bump Making two consecutive hand moves with the same hand (AKA going again).

Buttress A prominent rock face protruding from a crag.

C

Callouses	Areas of hard skin that can develop on the fingers or palm.
Campus Board	A training device that consists of a small overhanging board crossed by wooden rungs at regular intervals. The idea is to climb it without using the feet so as to develop arm and finger strength.
Campusing	Climbing without using the feet.
Centre of Gravity	The theoretical point where the entire mass of a body is concentrated (abbreviated to CoG).
Chalk	Magnesium Carbonate ($MgCO_3$) is a white powder that is used to absorb sweat from a climber's hands.
Chalk Bag	A small pouch for holding chalk that is hung on a belt tied around the waist.
Chalk Bucket	A large chalk bag designed to be left on the ground.
Chalk Ball	A small round mesh bag filled with chalk.
Chalking Up	Coating the hands with chalk.
Chicken Head	A protruding lump of rock, most common on granite.
Chicken Wing	A jamming technique in which the arm is bent and inserted into a crack elbow first with the palm pressed against one wall while the tricep/shoulder presses against the other. Similar to an arm bar.
Chipping	Creating or enhancing a climbing hold. The worst sin a climber can commit.
Cheatstone	A stone placed at the bottom of a problem to bring the starting holds into reach.
Chimney	A wide crack that is large enough to climb into.
Choss	Loose, dirty or otherwise unappealing rock.
Chunking	Breaking down a move or problem into small sections to figure out how to climb it.
Circuit	Either a grouping of problems of similar difficulty (most common in Fontainebleau, France) or a long problem, often a loop, climbed on an indoor wall to train endurance.
Climbing Shoes	Tight fitting, rubber covered shoes designed for rock climbing.
Cobble	An embedded stone that is used as a hold. Usually rounded and smooth.
Conditions	The suitability of the temperate, humidity, wind etc. for climbing.
Conglomerate	A sedimentary rock type that is mainly composed of embedded round stones (cobbles).
Compression	A technique for climbing symmetrical features by placing a hand (or foot) on either side and pulling hard to hold the body in place.
Core	The muscles of the stomach, lower back and legs.
Corner	A feature formed where two planes meet at roughly right angles (AKA dihedral).
Crag	A generic term for a climbing or bouldering area. May also refer specifically to an outcrop of rock.
Crimp	A small edge. Also a powerful grip in which the second finger joint is bent sharply and the thumb presses onto the index finger (AKA full crimp).
Cross Through	A traversing move in which one hand reaches past (over or under) the other to reach the next hold.
Crux	A problem's hardest move.

Cusp	A grip in which a protruding hold is squeezed, over the top or around the side, between the fingers and palm, with the fingers on the side nearest the body (AKA guppy).
Cutting Loose	When both feet swing off the rock and all the climber's weight is taken by the hands.
Crystal	A small piece of quartz that can be used as a hold, common on some types of granite.

D

Dab	When, mid ascent, a climber brushes off or hits into their spotter, a tree, the ground, another boulder or a pad.
Deadhang	To hang with straight arms without any assistance from the feet.
Deadpoint	The instant in a movement when the body is moving neither up nor down, the ideal time to grab a hold.
Deep Water Soloing	Climbing above water without a rope, often abbreviated to DWS.
Descent Route	The way down from a boulder (AKA downclimb).
Diagonal Stride	Using opposing limbs in coordination.
Down Climbing	Reversing down a problem either as a retreat or as a means of getting off a boulder.
Double Dyno	A dyno in which the target hold or holds are simultaneously grabbed with both hands.
Dropknee	When one foot inside edges while the other outside edges, the knee of the outside edging leg is lowered so that the feet are pushing away from each other rather than down (AKA Egyptian).
Dynamic	Any move that uses momentum.
Dyno	An all out leap during which the whole body is airborne and has, very briefly, no contact with the rock.

E

Edge	A flat horizontal hold.
Edging	Standing on an edge.
Eliminate	A contrived problem in which certain holds are deemed off limits to make the climbing harder.

F

Featured Wall	An indoor wall that is designed to resemble real rock.
Fingerboard	A small wooden or resin board covered in hand holds that is hung from to train finger strength.
Finger Jam	A jam in which the fingers are inserted into a crack and rotated until they are wedged.
Finger Tape	Strong tape designed to provide support to injured fingers.
First Ascent	The first time a boulder problem is climbed.
Figure Four	A very rarely used technique for making a long static reach from a positive hold. Involves hooking a leg over the holding arm.
Fist Jam	A jam in which the fist is inserted into a crack.
Flagging	To dangle one leg in the air for balance, usually done on steep rock.
Flake	A thin, partially detached, slice of rock.

Flapper | When a large chunk of skin is ripped off, usually during a dynamic move.

Flared | A crack with sides that taper outwards making it very difficult to jam.

Flash | To climb a problem on the first try from start to finish.

Fontainebleau | The famous bouldering area just south of Paris, France (AKA Font or Bleau). Also a system for grading boulder problems, the grade is often prefixed with 'Font'.

Footwork | The art of using the feet well.

Foot Cam | A technique in which the foot is rotated around the heel until it wedges, works well in horizontal cracks or breaks .

Foot Jam | A jamming technique in which the foot is wedged, toes first, into a crack.

Foot Swap | Replacing one foot for another on a foot hold.

Friction | The force created when skin or rubber is pressed into the rock.

Frogging | Getting the hips parallel and as close as possible to the wall with the knees pointing out to the sides.

Front Lever | A strength exercise that involves hanging from a bar, raising the body so it's horizontal and holding that position for as long as possible.

Front Pointing | Standing on a hold with the tip of the big toe.

Full-body Stem. | Climbing a very wide crack with the hands on one wall and feet on the other.

G

Gabbro | A coarse grained, rough igneous rock.

Gaston | Gripping a vertical hold with the arm bent at the elbow and the hand, thumb down, pulling the hold away from the body.

Golfer's Elbow | Aches and pains in the inside of the elbows caused by a lack of balance between the pushing and pulling muscles.

Grades | An indication of how difficult it is to climb a problem assuming good conditions and the best sequence.

Granite | A rough, igneous rock that consists mainly of quartz, mica, and feldspar.

Gritstone | A hard, coarse grained form of sandstone (AKA grit).

Groove | A shallow corner.

Ground Up | Attempting and climbing a problem or route without inspecting it from a rope and starting from the ground on each attempt.

Guidebook | A book containing information about a bouldering area (or areas) including details of the problems, directions, maps and photos.

H

Half Crimp | A versatile grip in which the fingers are partially bent. It's a compromise between open handing and crimping and is particularly useful on flat holds.

Hand Jam | A jam in which an open hand is inserted into a crack and pressed against the sides with the knuckles against one side, fingertips and palm against the other.

Hand Stacking | An advanced technique for hand jamming in offwidth cracks.

Headpointing | Climbing a route or problem after rehearsing the moves on a top rope first.

Heel Hooking | Placing the heel of the foot on a hold and using it like an extra hand.

Heel-toe jam | A jam used in wide cracks.

Highball | A tall boulder problem.

Hueco — A large rounded pocket.

I

Inside Edge — The straight edge running along the inside of the big toe.

Intermediate — A small hold that is used briefly during a reach to a distant hold.

J

Jamming — Wedging a body part into a crack.

Jug — A large incut hold (AKA bucket).

Jump — A dynamic movement in which one hand stays on while both feet leave the rock. There is at least one point of contact at all times.

Jump Start — Jumping from the ground to the starting holds of a problem (AKA French start).

K

Kipping — Kicking the legs to generate momentum when hanging from the arms.

Kneebars — A jam that leverages between foot and knee. The foot stands on a conventional hold while the knee (really the front or side of the lower thigh) presses into a corner, overlap or large protruding hold.

L

Lace Ups — Climbing shoes that are fastened with laces.

Landing — The landing zone beneath a problem.

Launch Pad — A small bouldering pad that is designed to protect the start of a problem or as a supplement to other larger pads.

Layback — A technique for climbing continuous vertical features such as cracks, flakes or aretes, that relies on opposition created by pulling with the hands and pushing with the feet (AKA liebacking).

Link Up — Combining sections or whole problems together to create a more difficult challenge.

Linking — Practising sections of a problem to prepare for the complete ascent from start to finish.

Limestone — A sedimentary rock composed of skeletal fragments of marine organisms such as coral.

Liquid Chalk — A mix of alcohol and chalk that is rubbed into the hands to coat them with chalk.

Lock Off — A static reach done with the holding arm bent sharply.

Lowball — A low or short boulder problem.

M

Mantel — A method of getting from hanging the lip of a boulder or ledge to standing on it (short for mantel-shelf). Also a verb, "mantel the ledge".

Matching — Placing both hands side by side on a hold (AKA sharing).

Midge — Tiny (1-4mm) flying insects which are most common in temperate climates during the summer months on humid, still days.

Mono — A small pocket that can only fit one finger.

Monzonite — An igneous rock type, similar to granite.

Morpho — A climb or move whose difficulty is highly dependent on the body shape or size of the climber. Usually code for "hard for the short".

N

No Hands Rest An excellent resting position that doesn't require the use of the hands.

O

Offwidth A crack that is too wide to jam but too narrow to climb inside.

Open Hand Gripping a hold with the fingers only slightly bent.

Opposition Creating tension either by pulling a pair of holds that face away from each other or pushing on a pair of holds that face each other.

Outside Edge The curved section of a climbing shoe between the tip of the big toe and the side of the little toe.

Over Gripping Holding on with the hands harder then necessary, wasting strength and energy.

Overhanging Rock that is steeper than vertical.

Overlap A small roof.

P

Palming Pressing the palm of the hand onto the rock.

Parkour A physical discipline that focuses on movement around obstacles by vaulting, rolling, running, climbing, and jumping (AKA free running).

Patioing Improving a landing by shifting rocks.

Pebbles Tiny stones protruding from the surface of the rock, most common on gritstone.

Pinch A hand hold that is squeezed between the fingers and thumb.

Pocket A hole in the rock that can be used as a hand or foot hold.

Power Endurance The ability to do multiple hard moves in a row.

Powerspot When the spotter takes some of the climber's weight so they can get the feel of a move.

Problem A bouldering route.

Pof Dried pine resin that is wrapped in a cloth and slapped onto hand and foot holds. It's used by a minority of climbers in Fontainebleau but most climbers consider it very damaging to the rock (AKA resin).

Project A problem that has been attempted but hasn't yet been climbed or a problem that an individual is working towards climbing ie. a personal goal.

Prow A narrow overhanging arete.

Pumped When the forearms become filled with lactic acid after a bout of hard or sustained climbing.

R

Reading Analysing how to climb a problem.

Red Herrings Holds that aren't essential to the sequence and only serve to distract and confuse.

Rockover Placing a foot on a high hold and standing up on it using a combination of pulling with the arms and pushing with the legs.

Roof An approximately horizontal piece of rock.

Rubber The sticky compound that is used on the soles of climbing shoes.

Run and Jump A dynamic technique that involves running at the rock, kicking off one or more foot holds and jumping for the hand holds.

S

Sandbag A problem that is given a significantly lower grade than it deserves. Also a verb, to sandbag, which is to underplay the difficulty of a problem.

Sandstone A sedimentary rock composed mainly of sand-sized minerals or rock grains.

Screw On A very small artificial hold, that is screwed rather than bolted to the surface of a climbing wall. Usually used as a foot hold.

Seam A narrow or closed crack.

Send To successfully climb a problem.

Sequence The details of how a problem is climbed (AKA beta).

Share To place both hands on the same hold simultaneously.

Sidepull A vertical hold that faces away from the body.

Sit Start To start a problem from a sitting position, sometimes abbreviated as SS or SDS (sit down start).

Slab A less than vertical piece of rock.

Slap A quick reach or lunge during which there is a minimum of two points of contact at all times.

Slippers Soft climbing shoes.

Sloper A rounded or sloping hand hold.

Slot A narrow horizontal pocket.

Smear A sloping foot hold. Used as a verb it means to place a foot flat against the rock.

Soloing Climbing a route without a rope. The complete term is free soloing.

Splitter A long, parallel sided crack.

Spotting Guiding a falling climber safely to the ground.

Sport Climbing Routes that are protected by clipping the rope to permanent bolts.

Sprag A grip in which the thumb pushes the rock above the fingers to create more downward force.

Squat An exercise for developing leg strength.

Squeak To thoroughly clean the sole of a climbing shoe.

Stalactites A limestone tooth that hangs from the ceiling of a roof.

Stamina The ability to do a large volume of climbing.

Static To do a move slowly and in total control.

Stemming Pressing the legs away from each other to create an opposition force that holds the body in place. Usually done in corners or grooves but can be done between two protruding holds (AKA bridging).

Stepping Through Standing (usually with the outside edge) on the next foot hold with the foot furthest from it.

Syenite A coarse grained igneous rock of similar composition to granite but with a very low amount of chalk.

Systems Board A steep board on which the various hold types - pinch, crimp, sloper, pocket, undercut, sidepull - are laid out in a repeating, symmetrical pattern.

T

Taco A type of bouldering pad that consists of one continuous section of foam that bends in the middle for transporting.

Technical A problem that demands a high standard of technique and movement skills.

Technique Can refer to either a specific type of movement or more generally to a climber's movement skills - "she has good technique".

Tennis Elbow Aches and pains in the outside of the elbows caused by a lack of balance between the pushing and pulling muscles.

Thumbcatch Improving a hold by pinching the underside of it with the thumb.

Tickmark A small chalk mark that indicates the location of a hard to see hold.

Toe Hooking Using the top of the toe to pull on a hold.

Topo A map or photo upon which the line taken by a problem (or problems) is marked.

Top Out The process of getting stood up on the top of a problem. Indoors you usually jump down from the finishing hold rather than top out.

Top Rope Anchoring the rope at the top of the cliff or boulder so that the climber can climb in safety.

Trad Climbing Climbing a route protected by gear that has been placed by the leader.

Training Board A small, steep wooden climbing wall (AKA woodie).

Traverse A problem that travels predominantly sideways.

Turning the Lip The process of getting from hanging from the lip of a roof to standing on the lip.

Tufas A limestone rib.

Twist-locking A technique for climbing steep ground in which the torso twists perpendicular to the rock to maximise reach.

U

Undercut A downward facing hold (AKA undercling).

V

V Grade An American system for grading problems, consisting of a number prefixed by the letter V, the higher the number the more difficult the problem.

Velcros Climbing shoes that are fastened with velcro straps.

Volcanic Tuff A rock type consisting of consolidated ash ejected from a volcano.

Volume A large, hollow plywood or resin hold (usually triangular or rounded), upon which other holds can be mounted.

W

Wall A roughly vertical piece of rock.

Warm-up A routine to prepare the mind and body for climbing.

Wire Brush A very aggressive wire bristled brush that should never be used to clean rock.

Wired Having a problem mastered (AKA dialled).

Working Figuring out and rehearsing the moves of a problem.

INDEX

GRADE COMPARISON TABLE

The table on the right is an attempt to compare the two major bouldering grading systems - the Hueco (or V) and Fontainebleau (or Font) - that are in use throughout the world today.

V grades are the standard in America, Australia and New Zealand, while Font grades are used in Europe, Asia and Africa.

There are many slightly different comparisons between the two systems, but none are considered definitive.

Generally the mapping between the scales is one to one but there are some exceptions, mostly in the lower and middle grades. At the higher grades, where grades are under such scrutiny, there is less confusion.

Comparing route and bouldering grades is very difficult, but the two rightmost columns should give route climbers some idea of what grade problems they may be able to climb.

One of the first bouldering grading systems was the B system. Invented by American bouldering legend John Gill in the fifties, it implicitly acknowledged the impossibility of absolute grading by expressing a problem's difficulty in terms of how many times it had been climbed. It was a simple scale with only three increments, B1 problems contained moves as difficult as those found on the hardest routes of the day, B3 was for problems that had only one ascent and everything in the middle was assigned B2.

This approach didn't stand the test of time and we now have the current systems with many increments and an illusion of accuracy.

V	Font	Route (UK)	Route (US)
V0	2+	VD	5.4
	3		
	3+	S	5.5
V1	4	HS	5.6
	4+	VS	5.7
V2	5	HVS	5.8
	5+		
V3	6A	.	5.9
	6A+	.	
V4	6B	.	.
	6B+	.	.
V5	6C		.
	6C+		.
V6	7A		.
V7	7A+		
V8	7B		
	7B+		
V9	7C		
V10	7C+		
V11	8A		
V12	8A+		
V13	8B		
V14	8B+		
V15	8C		
V16	8C+		

REFERENCES

GENERAL

Better Bouldering by John Sherman
Bouldering: Movement, Tactics and Problem Solving by Peter Beal
The Boulder: A Philosophy for Bouldering by Francis Sanzaro

EQUIPMENT

Alpkit - bouldering pads, chalk bags, down jackets - www.alpkit.com
Five Ten - climbing shoes - www.fiveten.com

MOVEMENT

The Self Coached Climber by Dan Hague, Douglas Hunter
Advanced Rock Climbing by John Long and Craig Luebben

TRAINING

Training for Climbing by Eric J. Hörst
Performance Rock Climbing by Dale Goddard, Udo Neumann
9 out of 10 climbers make the same mistakes by Dave MacLeod
How to Heal Elbow Injuries, www.ukclimbing.com/articles/page.php?id=3614
British Mountaineering Council Campus Board Guidance www.thebmc.co.uk/campusboard

HISTORY

John Gill: Master of Rock by Pat Ament
Full of Myself by Johnny Dawes.

GUIDEBOOKS

Yorkshire Gritstone Bouldering Volume 1 by Steven Dunning, Ryan Plews
Peak District Bouldering by Rupert Davies, John Coefield, Jon Barton
Boulder Britain by Niall Grimes
Essential Fontainebleau by John Watson
Boulder Albarracín by Desnivel
Crescianoboulder, Chironicoboulder, Gottardoboulder by A. Ambrosio, C. Cameroni, R. Grizzi, R. Lodi, N. Vonarburg
Swiss Bloc 1 by Gebro Verlag
Bishop Bouldering by Wills Young
Guidebook Hueco Tanks: The Essential Guide by Matt Wilder
Squamish Bouldering by Marc Bourdon
Comprehensive Castle Hill Climbing Guide by Matt Pierson, Alan Davison
Rocklands Bouldering by Scott Noy

ABOUT THE AUTHOR

David Flanagan is from Dublin, Ireland and has been climbing for nearly 20 years, focusing mostly on exploring and developing new bouldering problems and areas across Ireland. He has written and published a number of books including *Bouldering in Ireland*, *Rock Climbing in Ireland*, *Exploring Ireland's Wild Atlantic Way* and *Cycling in Ireland*.

ACKNOWLEDGMENTS

I owe a huge debt of gratitude to the following photographers who were kind enough to allow me reproduce their great photos.

Tobias Zlu Haller, Devlin Gandy, Paul Pritchard, Rolf Seitz, Troy Mattingley, Jeff Gardner, Jorge Crespo, Dan Varian, Thomas Burden, Tony Symanovich, Paul Bennett, Nick Brown, Christian Prellwitz, Simon McGovern, Daniel Schmid, Rudy Ceria, Peter McMahon, Fraser Harle, Steven Sloan, Ray Phung, Adam Long, Christophe Sahli, Nora Grosse, Keenan Takahashi, Erik Moore, Ian Parnell, Trish Fox, Alex Gorham, Susanica Tam, Richard Creagh, Ian Keirsey, Damon Corso, Lisa Robinson, Tom Hoyle, Diarmuid Smyth, Ryan Pasquill, Derek Thatcher, Matt Davis, Peter Wilkinson, Rowena Beaton, Simon Rawlinson, Eddie Gianelloni, Nic Mullin, Tim Haasnoot, Christine Ratcliffe, John Watson, Elly Stewart, Michal Madera, Ciaran Mulhall, David Mason, Brent La Fleur, Dirk Houghton, Dave Gater, Florian Oehrlein, Stefan Ösund, Rob Howell, Sebastian Smith, Beau Kahler, Aneta Parchanska, John Coefield, Pierre-Alexandre Pheulpin, David Rigaud, Reinhart Fichtinger, Seamus Allan, Marc Bourdon, Richard Tyler Gross.

Thanks to all the following who read the drafts, corrected mistakes and gave feedback.

Diarmuid Smyth, Chris Fryer, Simon McGovern, John Watson, Joe Morrison, Paul Daly, Niall Sheridan, Michael N, David Murray, Adan Vera, Marius Curtin, Karen Doyle, Ben Tyrrell, Simon Huthwaite, Howard Tingle, Trish Fox, Lorenzo Frusteri, Julie Flanagan, Brian Flanagan, Jenny Flanagan.

ABOVE David Flanagan on Split Arete, Poll Doo Glen. Donegal, Ireland. Photo by Peter McMahon.